Sabotaging the Planet:
Denial and International Negotiations

William McPherson
© 2016

Contents

Preface

Denial of climate change has consequences. As we have seen during the past four years, denial ideology has created a culture of political malfeasance, as politicians use denial to try to delay needed action. [1] While some politicians such as President Barack Obama have pressed ahead with regulations and negotiations to control carbon emissions, others have sought to stop the international community from taking action by reducing the role of the United States to a foot-dragger in negotiations. Much of this opposition began during the George W. Bush era when the administration sabotaged the implementation of the Kyoto Protocol.

This book investigates the consequences of denial for international relations. Climate change has both domestic and international implications: domestic, because virtually all policies are implemented at a national level; and international, because carbon emissions do not respect national borders. Emissions in any individual country will affect the global atmosphere.

Any individual country can sabotage an agreement on climate change when denial ideology there has a strong influence on its stance in negotiations. Of course, the largest emitters have more effects on the climate than small countries or those with fewer fossil fuel facilities. China and the U.S. are the largest emitters, accounting for about 45% of global emissions, and Chapter 1 examines the 2014 U.S.-China agreement for its effects on climate change negotiations. Other countries such as India and Brazil have lower emissions but are growing rapidly; they will also be discussed in Chapter 1. Whether any of these countries, or others, will sabotage the agreement is examined throughout the book, with particular emphasis on U.S. politicians who deny climate change.

A note on terminology: in the text and quotations you will encounter the expression "2C," which refers to two degrees Celsius (or Centigrade). It is shorthand for the criterion of global warming adopted in the Copenhagen Accord (2009) and the Cancun Agreements (2010), an increase in average global temperatures of 2C as a limit for global warming. Some scientists have also adopted this criterion as the basis for projecting "dangerous anthropogenic interference with the climate system,"[2] to quote the text of the climate agreement (more later). Research has indicated that "compared to unchecked global warming, keeping the temperature rise below 2C would reduce heatwaves by 89%, flooding by 76%, cropland decline by 41% and water stress by 26%."[3]

One indication of the challenge facing negotiations is that current projections of carbon emissions reveal that the world is likely to overshoot this 2C limit.[4] A British research institute, Grantham Institute, provided data on maximum emissions:

> The world can only emit a maximum 44 billion tonnes of carbon dioxide equivalent a year in 2030 to have a 50-66% chance of meeting that target, a report by the Grantham Institute said on Monday. The US, China and the EU, the world's top three emitters, will release some 22 billion tonnes annually by that date under published climate plans, depending on the year China's peaks its emissions. The rest of world is on track to emit an additional 35 billion tonnes, it found, clearly outstripping the target.[5]

"Published climate plans" refer to the Intended Nationally Determined Contributions (INDC) negotiated by parties to the UN Framework Convention on Climate Change, which will be discussed in detail in Chapter 3. They are one of the main components of the Paris Agreement that was negotiated during 2015. The Paris Agreement is the central focus of this book.

Chapter 1
International Negotiations on Climate Change

In 1992 the UN Framework Convention on Climate Change (UNFCCC) was signed at the Rio Summit (UN Conference on the Environment and Development) and the U.S. Congress ratified that agreement unanimously. The follow-up Kyoto Protocol (1997), however, was not ratified by the U.S. Congress and the U.S. is not a party to it.[6] Kyoto became a political football in U.S. politics because it was viewed as unfair since it only applied to developed countries. It was one of only a few international environmental agreements that had built in some sanctions. Member parties were expected to meet their targets or they could be assigned more stringent targets in the next period if they fell short. "Kyoto was the high-water mark for the idea of sanctions in climate agreements," said Alex Hanafi of the U.S. Environmental Defense Fund.[7] Lack of U.S. support made it likely that no future agreement would be feasible with sanctions, a consideration in the negotiations for the Paris Agreement. "The sting has been taken out of the process ... That means the chances of a deal are much better."[8]

UNFCCC has become the basis of the Obama administration strategy on international climate change policy. President Barack Obama has indicated that he does not need to submit further agreements to Congress. Because Congress had ratified the UNFCCC, it is now the "supreme law of the land" and further agreements under its auspices are valid. He is making a political calculation: that members of Congress would not ratify any further UNFCCC agreements submitted to it. He has suggested that those Congress members who deny climate change belong to a "Flat Earth Society."[9] There are plenty of members of that society, including a majority of members recently elected.

Other world leaders also recognize that an agreement must bypass the U.S. Congress to be successful: "We must find a formula which is valuable for everybody and valuable for the US without going to the Congress," said French Foreign Minister Laurent Fabius, who chaired the UN climate summit in Paris in December, 2015.[10]

Negotiations and ratification of the Kyoto Protocol portray the political nature of the UNFCCC. It was designed to implement a political clause of the UNFCCC, the "common but differentiated responsibilities" (CBDR) of the parties to reduce emissions. This phrase in the agreement has plagued the negotiations because it embodies all of the vexing issues of climate change:

- Developed countries, or "industrialized" members, have enjoyed 250 years of development at the expense of the atmosphere, using up more than half of the capacity of the globe to absorb carbon emissions before a 2C threshold is reached.

- Developing countries, particularly the "industrializing" members such as China, India and Brazil, are producing emissions at an exponential rate of increase. Their rapid rate of development depends on accelerated use of fossil fuels.

- The developed countries (in Annex I of the UNFCCC, which includes Europe, Russia, the U.S., Canada, Japan and Oceania) are expected to implement the agreement first while the developing countries are given a grace period. This is the provision that so offends Congress.

- Developed countries can try to buy their indulgences from developing countries through the "Clean Development Mechanism" (CDM) that earns credit for saving emissions through technology transfer between the developed and developing parties. The CDM has been widely abused by both developed and developing countries.

UNFCCC is basically an agreement by the nations of the world to control carbon emissions. Where does the carbon come from? Most is from industrialized or industrializing countries of the North, including China:[11]

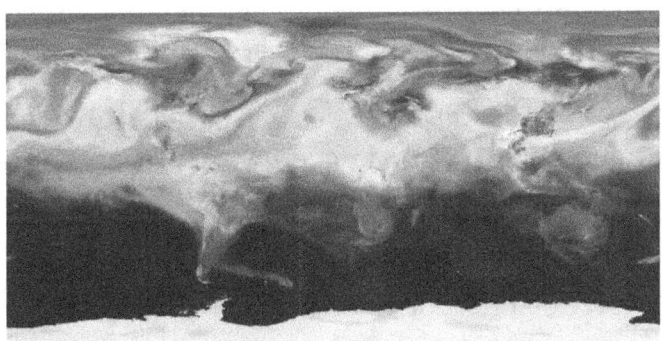

This map of the globe shows the heavy loading of emissions in the northern hemisphere, where most industrial activities take place. Southern hemisphere countries, which include most of the developing member parties of the UNFCCC, look to the north to reduce emissions first.

Most discussions of obligations of member parties are heated (pardon the pun), and various groups of countries such as the EU (European Union) and G-77 (developing countries) [12] take positions that are often subject to intense conflict. AOSIS (Association Of Small Island States) tends to take a strong position at the rapid decrease end of the spectrum while member parities with high emissions and/or oil wealth take a position at the other extreme. AOSIS, as you can imagine, has members whose countries may disappear with sea-level rise. The U.S., prior to the Obama administration, and others such as Saudi Arabia have often obstructed progress in the negotiations. The oil minister for Saudi Arabia, for example, said that climate action would "destabilize the global energy market" and his delegation opposed carbon pricing. [13] Whether the U.S. can continue its current support for progress depends on the outcome of future elections, particularly the 2016 presidential election. This uncertainty poisons the negotiations, particularly because of the stance of the U.S. Congress.

Negotiations since Copenhagen (2009) have stumbled over the necessity to renew or extend the Kyoto Protocol. At the Durban conference of parties of UNFCCC (2011), members decided to continue negotiations on two tracks, one seeking to extend Kyoto while the other is trying to come up with an entirely new agreement. These two tracks tend to overlap and then divide in varying meetings, as members try to reconcile many divisive issues. They mostly divide along the lines of developing and developed countries with the partial exception of the EU, which sometimes sides with developing country members.

Negotiations are plagued by political problems. The follow-on to the Copenhagen Accord (to limit warming to 2C) and the Cancun Agreements (that ratified the accord) are contentious over obligations to reduce emissions. According to scientists, it will be necessary over the next forty years to reduce greenhouse gas emissions to less than 2 tons per capita. This number is considered the necessary level of emissions to keep the temperature from rising above 2 degrees. The U.S. is at 20 tons, Europe is at 7.5 tons, Japan is at about 10, etc. All of these high-emissions countries have major battles over reducing emissions, both domestically and in formulating their international negotiation positions. Not only the total level is contentious, but also the pace of reduction is subject to intense fights.

What is the scale of the problem that international negotiators and policymakers face? "The world consumes roughly 1.3 trillion gallons of oil every year, along with 110 trillion cubic feet of gas, 17.6 trillion pounds of coal, and 2.4 trillion gallons of water. Resource challenges are denominated in billions and trillions. Any solutions must be able to scale."[14] Most of the remaining fossil fuel reserves must be left underground so the challenge of scaling back the trillions of gallons, cubic feet and pounds is enormous.

While all of the high-emissions nations have begun efforts to reduce emissions – with Europe at the foremost – they struggle to meet the targets they have already set. Scientists regard these targets as too weak, and are urging developed countries to set more ambitious targets. In addition, the question of whether developing countries will also set ambitious targets remains open. With China and the U.S. agreeing on moderate targets pressure will increase on the other high-emissions countries, especially Brazil and India, to follow suit.

U.S.-China Agreement

On November 12, 2014, President Barack Obama and Chinese President Xi Jinping agreed on cooperative action on climate change. Chinese President Xi said, "We agreed to make sure that international climate change negotiations will reach an agreement as scheduled at the Paris conference in 2015, and we agreed to deepen practical cooperation on clean energy, environment protection, and other areas."[15] The White House released a statement on the agreement that reads, in part:

> Today, the Presidents of the United States and China announced their respective post-2020 actions on climate change, recognizing that these actions are part of the longer range effort to transition to low-carbon economies, mindful of the global temperature goal of 2°C The United States intends to achieve an economy-wide target of reducing its emissions by 26%-28% below its 2005 level in 2025 and to make best efforts to reduce its emissions by 28%. China intends to achieve the peaking of CO2 emissions around 2030 and to make best efforts to peak early and intends to increase the share of non-fossil fuels in primary energy consumption to around 20% by 2030. Both

7

sides intend to continue to work to increase ambition over time. The United States and China hope that by announcing these targets now, they can inject momentum into the global climate negotiations and inspire other countries to join in coming forward with ambitious actions as soon as possible, preferably by the first quarter of 2015. The two Presidents resolved to work closely together over the next year to address major impediments to reaching a successful global climate agreement in Paris.[16]

As the last part of the statement indicates, the U.S. and China tried to influence other parties in the UNFCCC to make commitments before the meeting in Paris in late 2015. They succeeded, according to experts: "By showing the world's two largest economies are working together toward a common goal with different efforts, the breakthrough agreement signals greater global cooperation over the contentious issue. That eases tension that could help future global climate talks while also raising expectations for India to step up its efforts, experts and environmental activists say."[17]

China has indicated its interest in leading developing countries: Vice Premier Zhang Gaoli said: "We hope to enhance cooperation with developing countries in countering climate change, and offer our help and support for them."[18] Chinese government officials have acknowledged the severe effects of climate change on China: "As the world warms, risks of climate change and climate disasters to China could become more grave," said Zheng Guogang, the head of China's meteorological administration.[19] The U.S. and China cannot, by themselves, solve the climate problem but their agreement enhances the possibilities for action: "Climate change will not be solved only by the United States and China. But it certainly will not be solved without them," according to U.N. climate chief Christiana Figueres.[20] One expert offered this view of Chinese efforts: "Over the next 15 years, the Chinese will build enough clean electricity to power America."[21] If China can increase its renewable energy by that much, why not the U.S.? Considering the difference in population, the Chinese efforts are much more significant than those in the U.S.

Graphically, the U.S.-China agreement can be represented as follows:[22]

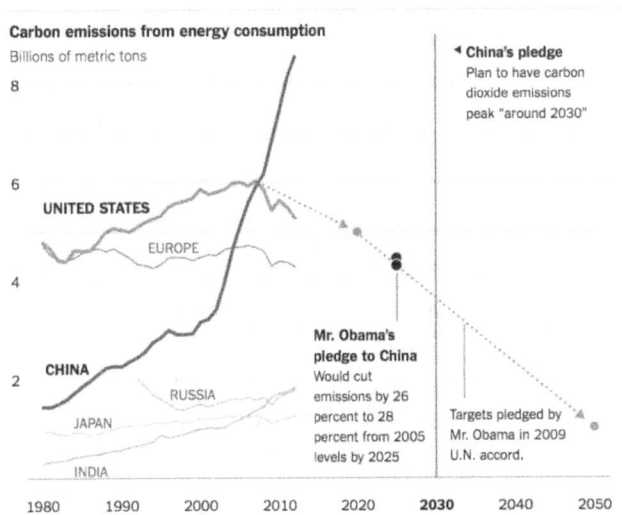

Carbon emissions from energy consumption
Billions of metric tons

◄ **China's pledge**
Plan to have carbon dioxide emissions peak "around 2030"

Mr. Obama's pledge to China
Would cut emissions by 26 percent to 28 percent from 2005 levels by 2025

Targets pledged by Mr. Obama in 2009 U.N. accord.

The question raised by this data is whether China can "bend" the curve showing its rapid increase in emissions. If indeed the emissions peak at 2030, they will have to decelerate before then and start a decline immediately thereafter. That is possible, as China is now the leading producer and installer of solar panels and wind turbines. [23] Its coal use is decelerating. Five provinces have instituted cap-and-trade systems and the government is rolling out a national cap-and-trade plan. China added 18 gigawatts of solar-energy capacity in 2015; China closed more than 200 of 523 coal plants since 2009; and coal usage in China declined by 21 percent since 2007. All of these will take time to slow the rapid acceleration now underway and bend the curve downward but the decline in the rate of emissions growth has started.[24]

Some politicians such as Senator Mitch McConnell have contended that the agreement gave

China a 15-year "free ride" to increase emissions, but the rate has to start declining now for the emissions to peak in 2030. Other politicians such as presidential candidate Donald Trump have pooh-poohed the Chinese climate program: "If you look at China, they're doing nothing about it."[25] Apparently Trump was not aware of the Chinese cap-and-trade program already underway in a number of Chinese cities and planned for the nationwide economy in 2017.

While some have hailed the U.S.-China agreement as a breakthrough because it enlists China in setting goals for the first time, others have pointed out that the goals set are woefully short of what is needed. Scientists have calculated that sustainable use of energy would limit emissions per capita to two tonnes (metric tons) per year worldwide. The U.S.-China agreement would allow up to 14 tonnes each after 2030 when all of the provisions take effect.[26] Instead of limiting temperature increases to 2 degrees, as agreed in Copenhagen, the U.S.-China agreement would result in increases of 4-5 degrees if emissions continued at these levels. The U.S. and China would then account for one-third of the total worldwide emissions, well above their proportion of the population today (about one fifth). They would be "crowding out" other countries, particularly developing countries. "At this level of emissions, the world will definitely cross the two degrees Celsius mark and go towards four-five degrees Celsius, unless India, Brazil, South Africa and all the rest of the emerging world stop their emissions right now. There is no space for the rest of the world after this deal."[27]

U.S.-Brazil Agreement

A meeting in June 2015 brought a joint announcement by Brazil and the United States in which "the two nations committed to increasing the use of wind, solar and geothermal energy to make up 20 percent of each country's electricity production by 2030, which would double power generation from renewable sources in Brazil and triple it in the United States. Brazil also pledged to restore about 30 million acres of Amazon rain forest, an area about the size of Pennsylvania."[28] This agreement is significant not only for the increase in renewable energy, but also the reforestation of the Amazon rain forest. Deforestation in the Amazon has been a major contributor to climate change.

Will these measures enable Brazil to meet its commitment of a 37% reduction of emissions by 2025 and a 43% reduction by 2030? Some Brazilian analysts have questioned that. "Those commitments seem too modest to reach the emission reductions they are proposing," said Britaldo Soares-Filho, an environmental modeling expert at the Universidade Federal de Minas Gerais.[29] As is the case with many member parties, Brazil has made ambitious commitments but is still working out the measures to meet them. Nevertheless, the commitments improved the prospects for agreement in Paris.

President Obama stated "Following progress during my trips to China and India, this shows that the world's major economies can begin to transcend some of the old divides and work together to confront the common challenge that we face – something that we have to work on for future generations."[30] He is building his legacy by making the U.S. an important player in the negotiations.

Why is the United States such an important player in these agreements? According to analysts of negotiations, the role of the U.S. is paramount: "the United States has greater diplomatic influence on other state actors and intergovernmental organizations than any other state," and "when the United States has been a veto state as in...the Kyoto Protocol, the result is a significantly weaker regime."[31] After the U.S. dropped out of the Kyoto Protocol, the UNFCCC became a weaker agreement and the negotiation of a follow-on agreement or protocol stretched out more than a decade. We are now at that critical point where the role of the U.S. will again become crucial. Whether domestic U.S.

politics will play a major role will be examined further in Chapter 2.

India

Some long-time observers of climate negotiations have taken hope from the U.S.-China and U.S.-Brazil agreements that India will follow suit. "I hope it will make India reconsider their strategy, and I see signs that the new Modi government is doing exactly this," said Connie Hedegaard, former EU climate chief.[32] The U.S. president's staff certainly thinks so: "Our...front burner issue is cooperation on clean energy and climate change...and the US, China, and India are key to this," said Phil Reiner, White House National Security Council senior director.[33] President Obama made climate change one of his major agenda items in his visit to India in January 2015. He admitted that the U.S. has had opportunities to grow without restrictions on carbon, but urged the Indians to join with other countries to reduce emissions.

> I know the argument made by some – that it's unfair for countries like the United States to ask developing nations and emerging economies like India to reduce your dependence on the same fossil fuels that helped power our growth for more than a century. But here's the truth: Even if countries like the United States curb our emissions, if countries that are growing rapidly, like India, with soaring energy needs don't also embrace cleaner fuels, then we don't stand a chance against climate change.[34]

As one of the most prolific and fastest growing emitters of greenhouse gases, India is a crucial partner in any international effort. But is India really a partner? At the time of this writing, it does not look like it. "If India goes deeper and deeper into coal, we're all doomed," said Veerabhadran Ramanathan, director of the Center for

12

Atmospheric Sciences at the Scripps Institution of Oceanography and one of the world's top climate scientists. "And no place will suffer more than India."[35] India has low-lying coastal areas that will flood with sea-level rise, and suffers major food shortages when droughts reduce agricultural productivity. Approximately 37 million Indians live in low-lying coastal areas.

While India may be concerned about the costs of switching from coal to renewable energy, they are more worried about the costs of adaptation to a changing climate. Zeenat Niazi, vice president of Development Alternatives, said that between 2015 and 2030 India will need at least $200 billion to adapt to the effects of climate change.[36] Although UNFCCC parties have pledged $100 billion a year after 2020, that may not be enough to cover India's costs when it is distributed among more than 100 developing countries.

In the run-up to Paris climate talks, India seemed to renege on its tentative steps to make commitments subject to verification by other parties. "Most significantly India and Saudi Arabia opposed the inclusion of a reference in the G20 statement to the need to discuss a 'review mechanism' that the EU and many economies say must be a central feature of the accord."[37] This "review mechanism" is a proposal by some member parties, particularly the EU, to subject the INDCs to five-year reviews after the initial commitment period.

Most significantly India and Saudi Arabia opposed the inclusion of a reference in the G20 statement to the need to discuss a "review mechanism" that the EU and many economies say must be a central feature of the accord. The accord is supposed to require all countries to volunteer pledges to cut their greenhouse gas emissions from 2020 or take other measures to tackle climate change.

India's approach to climate change seems to be, let others take the lead. We need to grow first. India's environment minister Prakash Javadekar said: "Whatever intentions have been declared by the US and China is a good beginning but it is not as ambitious as people wanted it to be."[38] While India waits to see what other countries do, it proceeds full speed with development. "India's development imperatives cannot be sacrificed at the altar of potential climate changes many years in the future," India's power minister, Piyush Goyal, said. "The West will have to recognize we have the needs of the poor." [39] This attitude reflects the oft-stated false dichotomy between poverty and climate policies. In fact, poverty will be exacerbated by climate change, not alleviated by fossil-fueled development. Perhaps the most succinct statement of this false dichotomy is by Sir Nicholas Stern: "We can now see that growth, development, mitigation, and adaptation go hand in hand, and that the portrayal of climate action as being in inexorable conflict with growth, poverty reduction, and radical improvements in human well-being is false and diversionary. Indeed, an attempt at high-carbon growth will self-destruct through the hostile physical environment it will create."[40]

Because India expects others to take the lead, it criticizes the U.S., whom it believes has not made strong enough commitments. According to Chandra Bhushan, the deputy director of the Centre for Science and Environment in New Delhi, "There's a general feeling within the government and outside that the U.S. [proposal] is very, very modest. It has not impressed the government of India. That is quite clear."[41] Bhushan was referring to the pledge by President Obama to reduce U.S. emissions by 26-28% by 2025 (with a baseline year of 2005), which pales in comparison to the EU pledge of 40% by 2030 (with a baseline year of 1990).

What energy policy is India pursuing vis-à-vis climate change? "Mr. Goyal has promised to double India's use of domestic coal from 565 million tons last year to more than a billion tons by 2019, and he is trying to sell coal-mining licenses as swiftly as possible after years of delay. The government has signaled that it may denationalize commercial coal mining to accelerate extraction."[42] "By 2030 India's coal consumption could triple or quadruple," according to Jairam Ramesh, minister of the environment under the previous prime minister, Manmohan Singh.[43] Coal is the most climate-intensive energy source and India's expansion of its use will overcome efforts of other countries, such as China, to address climate change.

Other Indian leaders agree with Mr. Goyal and Mr. Ramesh: "The growth of coal is inevitable," said Navroz K. Dubash, senior fellow at the Center for Policy Research in New Delhi. "India is still an energy-scarce society that is not able to keep the lights on in many parts of the country and still needs to build up much of its infrastructure. Given the energy needs, it is likely coal will grow — for how long and how much it's hard to say."[44]

Some observers disagree with the suggestion that India will not promote clean energy. "[Prime Minister] Modi absolutely believes, and he has publicly stated many times, that he wants to embrace the clean energy model. With Modi as prime minister we expect there will be a huge boost to this sector, because he not only talks, he also walks the walk," according to Krishnan Pallassana, executive director of The Climate Group India.[45] Modi had promoted solar power in Gujarat State when he was governor there. It looks as if he may apply that policy to the entire country. "In India, which has long been resistant to taking on its own climate change commitments, Prime Minister Modi recently tore up the country's target to install 20GW of solar capacity by 2022 and replaced it with a plan to build 100GW of projects by the same date – a move that could create up to 1 million jobs."[46] It will be necessary for India to find a low-carbon growth model; if it uses the "traditional carbon-intensive pathway," there is likely to be no credible possibility for all other countries to accomplish global carbon reduction.[47]

Other Countries

One of the consequences of the agreements among the U.S., China and Brazil is a reduction in demand for oil. Oil producers will have to take this agreement into account in marketing. John Browne, former chairman of BP, said "[The agreements] could reduce the two countries' cumulative oil demand by more than 17 billion barrels of oil over the next 15 years. But many operators remain largely insensitive to the potential consequences of such policies... [and few energy companies] publicly accept the science behind climate change and even fewer think of climate change as a risk to their business."[48] In this regard, oil producers are out of step with other businesses. Sir Richard Branson, CEO of the Virgin Airlines group, said "The politicians in Paris need to know business is behind them taking the right decisions and they are not going to damage the world economically by taking these decisions."[49]

A major issue for international negotiations is the degree of denial in member societies. While most of Europe seems to be firmly in the non-denial camp, the UK and some countries in eastern Europe have active denial campaigns. Outside Europe, there are denial groups in the U.S., Canada, and Australia[50] that may have some sway over those member parties' policies. In Australia, for example, former Prime Minister Tony Abbott has described the Green Climate Fund (see below) as "socialism masquerading as environmentalism." [51] Former Australian Treasurer Joe Hockey sneered a bit at U.S. President Obama's climate policies, saying "I just made the point that Barack Obama has to get any initiative on climate change through a hostile US Congress ... so far he hasn't had great success, you never know."[52] Hockey's comment shows how denial in the U.S. (see Chapter 2) can affect international views on negotiations.

Of course, not all Australians want to foot-drag on climate negotiations. Australian labor leader Bill Shorten said about Abbot "We've seen him furiously and desperately behind the scenes ask and shush and hush everyone from talking about climate change but unsurprisingly ... leaders of the rest of the world are determined to act on climate change ..."[53] Like opposition leaders in other countries (e.g., U.S. and Canada), Shorten is trying to fight domestic opposition to climate negotiations by referring to the efforts in the rest of the world.

Canadians also have their problems with denial. New Democratic Party Leader Tom Mulcair said, "To hear the Chinese saying they're ready now to discuss constraining limits on their greenhouse gas emissions, that's great news for the world. And Canada should be part of it. We're not."[54] Former Canadian Prime Minister Stephen Harper was more subtle in his comments: "It's not that we don't seek to deal with climate change. But we seek to deal with it in a way that will protect and enhance our ability to create jobs and growth, not destroy jobs and growth in our countries. And frankly, every single country in the world, this is their position. And that's why I've always been against a carbon tax or an emissions trading scheme because it harms our economy without necessarily helping the environment." [55] Harper is projecting his own views on other countries, but he has some validity with regards to the U.S. (see Chapter 2). Harper lost the election in November 2015, and the new prime minister, Justin Trudeau, may reorient Canadian policy away from the argument that emphasizes growth of jobs as the opposite of climate policies, a false dichotomy.[56]

United Kingdom (UK) voters seem to be solidly behind the government's climate policies, but there are groups in the UK that are skeptical. The UK Independence Party (UKIP) wants to scrap the UK climate change law and wants the UK to withdraw from the EU. Speaking about UKIP, Labor Party leader Ed Miliband said "There can be no ambiguity about our place in the European Union if we want to tackle climate change. If you are a party that is serious about climate change, you can't be a party that wants to leave the EU."[57] Of course, there are many reasons that voters who support UKIP candidates want to pull the UK out of the EU, but denial of climate change can be used to justify their position if they feel that the EU imposes too many energy regulations. Miliband's position is on the other end of the spectrum – he wants to reinforce UK participation in the EU and promotes success at the Paris negotiations. "We want the Paris summit to be a big moment when the world says this matters for our kids and for their kids. There is no choice but for this movement to be successful."[58]

Some columnists in the United States have tried to analyze the impact of denial on the U.S.-China agreement. "Agreements like this are more important than they might appear at first glance, because in both countries there are political factions that justify inaction by pointing at the failures of the other country."[59] China does have factions that may oppose the agreement, but they are unlikely to have much effect. The U.S. has the most active and influential denial movements, and their influence on Congress is robust.

Chapter 2

Denial and Congress

Action on climate change tends to arouse opposition from denial ideologues. Although President Obama and President Xi agreed on climate policies, leaders of Congress found reasons to object. Senator Mitch McConnell (R-KY), majority leader of the Senate, said "This unrealistic plan that the president would dump on his successor, would ensure higher utility rates and far fewer jobs." [60] He also said "I read the agreement - requires the Chinese to do nothing at all for 16 years while these carbon emission regulations are creating havoc in my state and other states around the country."[61]

Is McConnell correct in saying the Chinese will do "nothing at all for 16 years?" Here is what the Chinese are doing: "At the 2013 Communist Party Plenum, China's leaders committed to reduce coal's share of primary energy below 67 percent by 2017 by implementing higher resource taxes or caps on coal use. In November 2014, China's State Cabinet released details of plans to cap coal consumption at 4.2 billion tons in 2020, a limit that will require severe cuts in coal use in Beijing and other large coal-dependent regions."[62] In one respect, McConnell has a point – the agreement does not require China to do as much as the U.S. in the next 15 years – but he conveniently overlooks the division between developed and developing countries built into the UNFCCC agreement. That agreement was, after all, unanimously ratified by the Senate in 1992 when McConnell was a member.[63]

McConnell undermined the U.S. delegation to Paris when he directly attacked the U.S. position in international negotiations, contending that the U.S. could not make commitments to reduce emissions that would survive domestic opposition. "Even if the job-killing and likely illegal Clean Power Plan were fully implemented, the United States could not meet the targets laid out in

19

this proposed new plan. Considering that two-thirds of the U.S. federal government hasn't even signed off on the Clean Power Plan and 13 states have already pledged to fight it, our international partners should proceed with caution before entering into a binding, unattainable deal."[64] While the president was in Paris to lead U.S. negotiators in attaining an agreement, McConnell said, "The next president could simply tear it up. Governments currently engaged in this round of climate talks will want to know that there is more than just an Executive Branch in our system of government," [and the climate agenda] "may not even survive much longer anyway."[65]

McConnell's statements illustrate two problems posed by denial ideology for international negotiations: (1) The implementation of international commitments depends on domestic support, which can be undermined by politicians, and (2) the perception of weakness by one party can reduce the commitments of other parties. McConnell is doing his utmost to sabotage the agreement by generating doubts about the U.S. commitments.[66] He has sent a letter to some foreign leaders in which he suggests that the U.S. will not honor its commitments under future presidents. He calls the administration's position a "house of cards." [67]

Senator James Inhofe (R-OK), chairman of the Senate Environment Committee, complained that China will increase its emissions until 2030 and then argued that the agreement would impose a $300 billion "tax" on the U.S. economy.[68] Inhofe also said, "Even if they did agree to reducing emissions, we wouldn't believe them. They don't end up doing what they say their going to do in these agreements." [69] He considers the Obama administration policies as "reckless" and misleading the world: "The president and his State Department officials are recklessly leading the world to believe we will live up to emission reductions the administration can't substantiate and won't even defend before congressional committees."[70]

When President Obama pledged $3 billion for the Green Climate Fund, an international effort to help developing countries adapt to climate change, Senator Inhofe said, "President Obama's pledge to give unelected bureaucrats at the U.N. $3 billion for climate change initiatives is an unfortunate decision to not listen to voters in this most recent election cycle. The president's climate change agenda has only siphoned precious taxpayer dollars away from the real problems facing the American people. In a new Congress, I will be working with my colleagues to reset the misguided priorities of Washington the past six years."[71] His sentiments were echoed by Representative Morgan Griffith (R-VA): "When [Mr. Obama] makes promises of billions of dollars, a lot of nations ought to take that with a grain of salt because that money may not be there."[72] If Inhofe and Griffith are successful in resetting what they call *"misguided priorities,"* they may alienate many of the UNFCCC member parties whose support of international efforts is crucial. That would be as misguided as anything Congress could do to sabotage negotiations.

Inhofe is dead set against any U.S. support for a Paris Agreement. "For those who believe there really will come into effect in Paris a treaty – and the president has said that will happen – you should keep in mind this is something that isn't going to happen. The American people are not ready. They have already studied this issue. They know the science is not there. What they want to do is to avoid any kind of negative effect on our economy and that is exactly what I think will happen."[73] Climate science is a problem for Inhofe, because it shows trends toward global warming that Inhofe does not want to admit.[74] When he says that science is *"not there,"* he apparently means it is not where he wants. He prefers that science abnegate findings of temperature increases. That would not be possible given the facts on which science must base its findings.

Inhofe infamously threw a snowball on the Senate floor to "prove" that there is no global warming. Of course, Inhofe is using weather to try to refute climate, which is measured on a much longer time frame.

In addition, Inhofe uses one of the canards of denial ideology to justify his rejection of international agreements on climate change. "While some Democrats may be convinced that global warming is continuing to occur, the scientific record does not agree. In fact, for the past 15 years, temperatures have not increased."[75] *"Have not increased"?* Inhofe also claims that the globe is cooling.[76] It seems that Senator Inhofe has not paid attention to the facts:

Top 10 Warmest Years (1880–2014)

The following table lists the global combined land and ocean annually-averaged temperature rank, and anomalies from the 134-year average, for each of the ten warmest years on record.[77]

RANK 1 = WARMEST PERIOD OF RECORD: 1880-2014	YEAR	ANOMALY °C	ANOMALY °F
1	2014	0.69	1.24
2 (tie)	2010	0.65	1.17
2 (tie)	2005	0.65	1.17
4	1998	0.63	1.13
5 (tie)	2013	0.62	1.12
5 (tie)	2003	0.62	1.12
7	2002	0.61	1.10
8	2006	0.60	1.08
9 (tie)	2009	0.59	1.06
9 (tie)	2007	0.59	1.06

Every one of the record years except 1998 are in the 21st Century, which is on track to be much warmer than the 20th Century. At the time of this writing, NOAA reported that 2015 is likely to be even warmer than 2014.[78] Thus it seems that Senator Inhofe is wrong in citing the last 15 years as a period when temperatures have not warmed. Like many denial ideologues, he mistakes a slowdown in the warming trend for a reversal. Inhofe is relying on ideology rather than science for his denial of facts.[79]

Politicians like Inhofe often claim that the globe is cooling. Based on natural climate cycles, the globe *should* be cooling, as we are in a period of less solar activity than before the 1980's. If we look at the natural climate variability and compare it to actual temperature records, we have to conclude that human activity is responsible for all of the recent warming: "the underlying long-term trend for the Earth – driven largely by changes in our orbit – has been a very slow cooling. Human activity has overwhelmed all of these trends."[80] If one ignores human causes of climate change, one could conclude that the earth is cooling, but as we have seen in the temperature records (above), that conclusion is wrong, much as politicians would prefer to ignore the data.

Sometimes the false denial claim of a reversal of global warming is based solely on misreading atmospheric temperatures. While the atmospheric warming has slowed, it has not stopped; further, the oceans are warming rapidly as the following data from IPCC indicates:

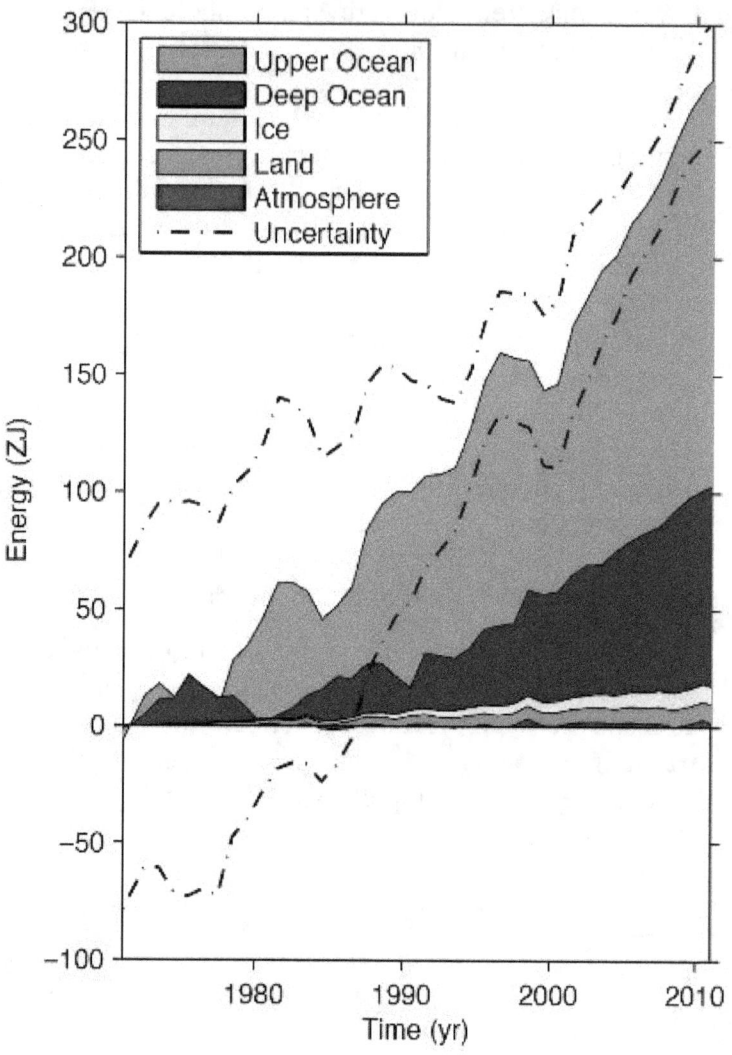

While increases in atmospheric temperature have slowed (as indicated by the lowest curve), the overall increase including ocean temperature has not. As can be seen from the data, the false assertion that the globe is cooling, or not warming, has no basis in fact. Nevertheless, U.S. politicians continue to base their decisions and evaluations of international agreements on misinformation.[81]

Other statements by politicians also are based on misinformation. Regarding the U.S.-China agreement, Senator John Barasso (R-WY) said "To me, this is an agreement that's terrible for the United States and terrific for the Chinese government and for the politicians there, because it allows China to continue to raise their emissions over the next 16 years." [82] Barasso, like McConnell, misused terms of the agreement to imply that the Chinese are not going to do anything for 16 years. In contrast, Senator Lindsay Graham (R-SC) said, "I'm positive about trying to cooperate with China on this. We'll see."[83]

Former Speaker John Boehner (R-OH) said, "This announcement is yet another sign that the president intends to double-down on his job-crushing policies no matter how devastating the impact for America's heartland and the country as a whole."[84] It is perhaps accidental irony that Boehner used the term *"heartland,"* which is the name of the Heartland Institute, a leading climate change denial organization.[85] Boehner pledged that Republicans "would continue to make blocking Obama's energy policy a priority for the rest of his term."[86]

Lamar Smith (R-TX), chairman of the House Science, Space and Technology Committee, said "President Obama negotiated a deal to tie our economy's hands while driving up energy costs for hardworking American families. I fail to see how this agreement benefits the United States. China has not promised to do anything other than increase its own energy production at unprecedented rates. Why would the president boast about an agreement where the American people come up with the short end of the stick?"[87] Smith does not explain how *American people come up with the short end of the stick* when they might actually benefit from reducing emissions regardless of what China does.

One member of the House, Representative Tom Cole (R-OK), suggested one way that the Congress could try to block Obama: "You can issue all of the executive orders you want. If you don't have any money to enforce them, they don't go very far. We're going to be pretty aggressive in using the power of the purse." [88]

Republicans have already succeeded in getting limits on EPA funding written into the budget agreement for fiscal year 2015. They made attempts to extend this limitation in the omnibus budget that runs through March 2017. These attempts, however, have not stopped the EPA rules on power plants (see below).

Politicians running for president are not all members of Congress. One who took an early lead in the polls in the Republican race was Donald Trump, the billionaire real estate mogul. He did not indicate outright denial of climate science but commented on the U.S.-China agreement: "the concept of global warming was created by and for the Chinese in order to make U.S. manufacturing non-competitive."[89] He indicated that he was being sarcastic, but like many of Trump's statements one cannot be sure.

This is only the opening round of charge and counter-charge of U.S. political bickering over climate change. The U.S. political system has built-in mechanisms that insure conflict. While a majority of the population supports climate action, they are not represented in Congress because of gerrymandering in the House (abetted by the large number of Republican-controlled state governments) and the disproportionate number of Senators from small states. A majority of voters in 2014, for example, voted for candidates for Senate who supported climate action. But because small states like Wyoming can send as many senators to Washington as the large states as California, the Senate is 54-46 Republican. More than 60% of these Republican senators are climate deniers. While a majority of the majority supports climate action, Congress can block it. This is a recipe for gridlock, not a good sign for climate action.

Denial in the U.S. political system is supported by a major industry of climate denial hucksters. These ideologues have developed a suite of false arguments about "natural climate change," "global cooling" and "drastic economic damage" to feed politicians' need for avoidance of action.[90] The resistance to international action is growing in the U.S. political establishment (outside the Obama administration, which is fighting a rear-guard battle). States are finding ways to infuse climate denial in their educational systems and energy policies.[91]

U.S. Politicians' Denial and Negotiations

How does this resistance affect international negotiations? It remains be seen if the Paris Agreement will be any more effective than the Kyoto Protocol. Its implementation depends heavily on domestic actions by all member parties. If the U.S. backslides after 2016, the rest of the world will be less dedicated to carrying any commitments to emission reductions. "It is not certain how the US will deliver the 2025 targets – one year after Paris, Obama will be out of office," according to Connie Hedegaard, outgoing climate chief for the EU.[92] Of course, the EU has been skeptical of U.S. intentions since the negotiation of the Kyoto Protocol. As well-informed observers have noted, "Congress has remained a force for reducing US leadership" in climate negotiations.[93] French President François Hollande alluded to Congressional opposition: "I know that the United States has difficulties with its Congress, which is perfectly understandable, and I know how difficult it is. But we must give the agreement in Paris – if there is an agreement – a binding nature, insofar as the commitments that will be made have to be honored and respected."[94]

Will the U.S. backslide after 2016? If a Republican wins the presidency, it is quite possible. "Republicans do not want to be targeted by conservative outside groups like Americans for Prosperity, the political advocacy group funded by the libertarian billionaires Charles and David Koch. Tim Phillips, the president of Americans for Prosperity, has said that his group intends to aggressively attack any Republican candidate in the 2016 primaries who endorses carbon regulations."[95] But some Republican strategists worry that the position on climate change that could help win them their party's nomination could hurt them in the 2016 general election, particularly in a contest with a larger number of young and minority voters. [96] The outcome of the election depends on turnout of the young and minority voters, and that in turn depends on their view of the efficacy of the government in managing climate change.

While the Obama administration has set some goals for reductions of emissions, there needs to be follow-up implementation to realize these goals – particularly the reduction of 28% by 2025. Future administrations will have to maintain the integrity of the EPA regulations on power plants and the mileage standards of U.S. vehicles to attain these goals.

Congress and other U.S. politicians will be particularly attuned to any lack of commitment by other countries. The "free rider" hazard is particularly acute in climate change. If China and the U.S. succeed in reducing their emissions by 2030 as planned, will other countries do likewise? Will India and Brazil follow through on their commitments? If not, then Congress and state governments will have every excuse not to carry out the U.S. commitments. The state governments are particularly important because of the nature of EPA regulations on power plants. The states have the leading role in implementing those regulations.

Congress is already predisposed to deny climate science, or at least pander to the Republican Tea Party base that is adamant about denying climate science. When the U.S. Senate was voting on the Keystone XL Pipeline in January 2015, Senator Bernie Sanders (I-VT) introduced amendments to force senators to vote on climate science. He characterized the opposition as follows: "I think some of them – Jim Inhofe who I like and is a friend of mine is very sincere in his belief that climate change is a hoax, who absolutely believes that. But I think there are other senators who do not believe that. There are other senators who have scientific backgrounds but for political reasons are not prepared to come out and say that climate change is real."[97]

Whether the senators genuinely deny climate science or support those who do, they have the same effect on U.S. positions in international negotiations. Congress can undercut U.S. diplomats by raising questions about U.S. commitments. Other diplomats are likely to keep their eyes on U.S. domestic politics while discussing proposals with U.S. diplomats.

Some politicians have gone way out in their denial of climate science. At times this takes the form of condemning government agencies that fund the science. Rep. Jeff Duncan (R-SC), said:

> I think that we've got threats of ISIS; we've got cartels shooting at helicopters on the border; we've got unaccompanied children coming into this country; **we've got illegal aliens murdering beautiful innocent lives in San Francisco; we've got a woman who had her head blown off in Los Angeles by someone. There are events after events going on around the world that are true threats to the United states, folks who want to do great harm to Christians, want to do great harm to others.** They want to come to this country and end the American way of life, and for whatever reason, we're now spending out hard-earned dollars on climate science and the belief that this is one of the biggest threats to national security.[98]

While somewhat extreme, this statement reflects the view that climate change is not a threat, and that climate science should be treated as a low priority in government funding or be cut off completely. Such a view conflicts with the view of scientists and politicians who see it differently.

With regard to the Paris Agreement, Senator Barrasso (R-WY) made a number of objections to the agreement. He claimed that the agreement "won't achieve the environmental gains that have been promised." Overlooking the fact that many developing countries are making pledges, including China, he said they "are getting a pass on having to take any shared economic pain." [99] Barrasso is also frustrated that the Obama administration is treating the Paris Agreement as an executive agreement, because it does not require Senate approval. He said "whatever deal is reached in backrooms of the Paris climate change conference, it has been telegraphed by this Administration that the deal will be a calculated end-run around Congress." [100] This issue has cropped up in a number of Congressional statements, but the Senate did unanimously ratify the UNFCCC. Once ratified, it has the force of law and the administration is compelled to reduce emissions that are a "dangerous anthropogenic interference with the climate system," to quote the language of the agreement.

Senator Shelly Moore Capito (R-WV) sought to defund the U.S. contribution to the Green Climate Fund. She also indicated that opposition by U.S. states (see below) could undermine the Obama administration's climate goals: "In my opinion, they are inextricably tied to the upcoming climate negotiations. President Obama cannot meet his goal of 28 percent reduction in CO_2 emissions without the full implementation of this regulation." [101] She is referring to an EPA regulation to require reductions in emissions, a regulation that could result in closing coal power plants. Like many coal state politicians, Capito is fighting against the regulation. She warned negotiators that the U.S. would not be likely to comply with the Paris Agreement. "World leaders should be cautious about entering into a deal with an administration whose misguided policies lack the backing of a bipartisan majority in Congress." [102]

Representative Lamar Smith (R-TX, chairman of the House Committee on Science, Space and Technology, said employees of NOAA (National Oceanic and Atmospheric Administration) "altered historical climate data to get politically correct results in an attempt to disprove the 18-year lack of global temperature increases."[103] He contends that "climate alarmists" are trying to refute the claim that there is a "hiatus" in global temperature increases by doctoring the data. He said that NOAA had been rushing its analysis to publish it in advance of the Paris talks.

What is the net result of all of this conflict and denial? American politicians are always talking about oil, coal, jobs, "climate alarmism," economic decline and their own lack of scientific expertise.[104] What they should talk about is heat, storms, drought, floods and extreme weather.[105] By changing subjects to exclude topics they do not want to include in the national conversation, the politicians are misdirecting American society away from the issues that need to be discussed toward dead-end issues. They need to look at the future in terms of what has to be done to face the reality of climate change.

EPA Rules

One area of U.S. policies that arouses vehement political opposition is coal plant rules. EPA (Environmental Protection Agency) is a frequent target of politicians who want to restrict federal government funding and/or action on climate change. EPA is now developing its rules on coal-fired power plants:

> In this action, the Environmental Protection Agency (EPA) is proposing emission guidelines for states to follow in developing plans to address greenhouse gas emissions from existing fossil fuel-fired electric generating units. Specifically, the EPA is proposing state-specific rate-based goals for carbon dioxide emissions from the power sector, as well as guidelines for states to follow in developing plans to achieve the state-specific goals. [106]

Goals vary by state, depending on current power plant emissions, from as low as 215 tons emissions per megawatt-hour in Washington State (which has mostly hydropower and wind power, and thus little scope for reductions) to 1800 in Wyoming. The average is about 1100 tons.

Nearly all fossil-fuel power plants are fired by coal or natural gas. Gas-fired plants would meet the rules easily but coal-fired plants would not unless equipped with carbon capture and storage (CCS), which is only used on pilot plants now. CCS is energy-intensive, taking nearly 40% of the power produced by the plant to operate. It makes coal-fired plants uneconomical. As a result, most coal-fired power plants are likely to close when this rules take effect.

As can be imagined, resistance to the rules is particularly intense in coal states such as Kentucky, where Senator McConnell was elected on a platform of fighting against the alleged "war on coal." [107] How Kentucky and other coal states can implement the rules is an open question and one that will plague enforcement of the rules by EPA even if they take effect.

The state-by-state nature of the rules was designed to let the state governments find the best way to implement them, but it also has a political side effect: the states can develop strategies to evade enforcement and the EPA may not be able to overcome all of them. The crunch will come when the rules are enforced and states react, most likely with lawsuits or other means of opposing the rules. Texas has already sued EPA over its use of the Clean Air Act to regulate greenhouse gases from power plants. Other states may follow suit.

Politicians have also latched on to this state-by-state administration of the EPA rules. Senate Majority Leader Mitch McConnell said "Think twice before submitting a state plan ... when the administration is standing on shaky legal ground," implying that the EPA rules could be overturned by Congress or the courts.[108] EPA Administrator Gina McCarthy responded, "For a rule like this there is no way that we are not going to be challenged. We think we have appropriately used 111-D for this sector and that the rule will be not just be legally defensive, it's going to be solid."[109] 111-D refers to the section of the Clean Air Act under which EPA issues the rules on carbon emissions.[110]

McConnell's call on states to resist EPA rules has borne fruit in many states with Republican governors. "As governors begin to seriously look at what these plans will look like, we expect more and more governors will follow Senator McConnell's lead," said Robert Steurer, a spokesman for McConnell.[111] Several governors made their agreement with McConnell explicit.

- Texas governor Greg Abbott said "The E.P.A.'s latest attempt at imposing burdensome regulations represents an unprecedented meddling with Texas in order to push the Obama administration's liberal climate change agenda."[112]

- Louisiana: Michael Reed, a spokesman for Louisiana Governor Bobby Jindal, said: "The president's Clean Power Plan undermines the role of states in the federal Clean Air Act in an effort to realize a radical, liberal agenda that will lead to increased energy costs. While we believe the proposed rule should be immediately withdrawn, we are considering all options to mitigate the damage if it becomes final, including not submitting a plan."[113]

- Wisconsin: In a letter to Mr. Obama, Wisconsin Governor Scott Walker wrote that he feared the "staggering costs it would inflict on Wisconsin's homes and businesses," and added that "it is difficult to envision how Wisconsin can responsibly construct a state plan."[114]

With these statements and possible follow-up actions, states can undermine the position of the Obama administration in the UNFCCC negotiations. Other states whose governors that have indicated that they will ignore EPA rules include Indiana, Oklahoma and West Virginia. Their efforts may be in vain, however. "What's really on all of the governor's minds is that they have an opportunity to tailor a plan to meet local conditions. But they don't really have an opportunity to shield the power companies in their state, because if the states don't do regulate the power plants, it's a federal responsibility to do it."[115]

EPA will have the backing of a majority of the U.S. public. In the runup to the Paris Agreement (Chapter 5), polling indicated that nearly two-thirds of the public supported a strong agreement and EPA rules. "Two-thirds of Americans support the United States joining a binding international agreement to curb growth of greenhouse gas emissions, but a slim majority of Republicans remain opposed, the poll found. Sixty-three percent of Americans – including a bare majority of Republicans – said they would support domestic policy limiting carbon emissions from power plants."[116] This support will be crucial to successful U.S. implementation of the pledges it has made during the negotiations for the Paris Agreement. Still, there are those who would undermine the U.S. pledges using denial ideology.

During the 2016 presidential campaign, the issue of power plant regulation came up, and most Republican candidates opposed the Obama administration's rules. "Sadly, although a majority of Republican voters support regulating carbon as a pollutant, and a plurality even support President Obama's Clean Power Plan, the party's leaders have now taken an extreme stance on the issue. Many of the party's presidential candidates deny that the planet is even warming (e.g. Ted Cruz), or that humans are responsible (e.g. Donald Trump, Ben Carson, Jeb Bush, Marco Rubio, John Kasich). Among those few who accept the scientific consensus, most oppose all practical efforts to address the problem (e.g. Chris Christie, Carly Fiorina)," according to one observer.[117] With this list of possible presidents, it is not a certainty that the EPA rules will survive the Obama Administration.

One Congressman in an influential position, Ed Whitfield (R-KY), chairman of a subcommittee with oversight of EPA, contended that the Obama administration is simply trying to burnish the president's legacy. "Why is EPA, at the direction of the president, rushing it through? EPA obviously wants this completed before the 2016 elections. Is it being done to create a legacy in the international arena for President Obama?"[118] Whitfield used the occasion of EPA rulemaking to criticize the Obama administration for its negotiations, just as Obama was trying to build support for the Paris Agreement. Obama made the following statement about U.S. leadership in the climate negotiations:

> Climate change can no longer be denied – or ignored. The world is looking to the United States – to us – to lead. Today, there's no greater threat to our planet than climate change. This is the only planet we've got. And years from now, I want to be able to look our children and grandchildren in the eye and tell them that we did everything we could to protect it.[119]

As Whitfield implied, Obama was talking about legacy, but not the way Whitfield suggested. Obama's concept of legacy is not the reputation of his presidency, but the future of world society. When the EPA released a report in June, 2015, the White House reinforced EPA rules with the a statement that indicated the value of the rules for the U.S. negotiators: "That's what we're going to use to push other countries to join in global climate action."[120]

Because the EPA rules and other administration actions depend on the president's authority, congressional opponents talk about using the "power of the purse" to stymie them. "You can issue all the executive orders you want. If you don't have any money to enforce them, they don't go very far," said Rep. Tom Cole (R-OK) "We're going to be pretty aggressive in using the power of the purse."[121] Regarding the EPA rules, Congress may try to limit money for enforcement. This would make the rules less effective in limiting emissions.[122]

This is another example of the misdirection of American politics away from the crucial issues of climate change – the need for sustainable energy and adaptation to storms, floods, droughts and extreme weather – toward regulations. The EPA may be carrying out the best policies for climate change, or there may be a need for improvement, but the approach needed is to look at how effective these policies are, not whether they are necessary – which is a given.

Of course, their effectiveness will arouse more opposition, the more effective they become. Already, Senate Majority Leader McConnell has indicated his hostility: "They've been on a rampage all across the country. And I think coal is the most conspicuous example, but it's happening in a lot of other areas and I think you're going to see bipartisan support for trying to rein them in."[123] If McConnell means stopping the EPA from enforcing the Clean Air Act, he may find it difficult to *rein them in.* The Clean Air Act has been upheld in court decisions and while enforcement is always problematic, non-governmental bodies can reinforce its effect. U.S. environmental law allows non-governmental bodies to bring lawsuits if the government is slacking off in enforcing the law, and it is highly likely that will happen in climate policy cases.

All of this conflict is happening at the domestic level in the U.S., while diplomats attempt to negotiate an international agreement to manage climate change. Whether the U.S. political conflict affects international action, however, will depend on future positions taken by the U.S. in the next administration(s). Unless the president elected in 2016 upholds EPA rules, they may be discarded or weakened to the extent that they have little effect on U.S. emissions.

Chapter 3
Negotiation of the Paris Agreement: Preliminaries

"It's very important that we get strong and effective outcomes from the conference in Paris [in 2015]. It is a subject that the world needs to tackle as a whole. We all are doing what we can, Australia as well, and we need a strong and effective agreement from Paris. I think it's very important that we don't have another disaster like Copenhagen and it's vital that the Paris Conference be a success, unlike Copenhagen." French President Francois Hollande[124]

In the following discussions of international negotiations, statements of some of the high-emitting UNFCCC parties such as the United States, China, Japan, Brazil, South Africa, Europe and India will be featured. Their emissions are the most important issue in the negotiations, and the approach they take (and responses from other member parties) will be crucial for the success of the negotiations. Coupled with discussion of the diplomatic moves is a review of some of the denial statements linked to the negotiations.

Negotiations in Lima, Peru

UNFCCC uses a nomenclature of "COP" for Conference of Parties and designates each with a serial number. The twentieth Conference of Parties in Lima was labeled COP20. What was unique about COP20 in Peru? Together with COP 21 in Paris, these negotiations were the first in which all parties pledged to make commitments of Intended Nationally Determined Contributions (INDC) for emission reductions. Previously, under the Kyoto Protocol, only industrialized member parties made such commitments. Another feature is setting goals for 2050 such as net-zero emissions by then. Together, these two parts of the Paris Agreement will be the most significant advances over previous agreements.

An example of INDCs is the U.S. commitment. As noted in Chapter 1, the U.S. has committed to reducing emissions by 26-28% below 2005 levels by 2025. This can be represented graphically:

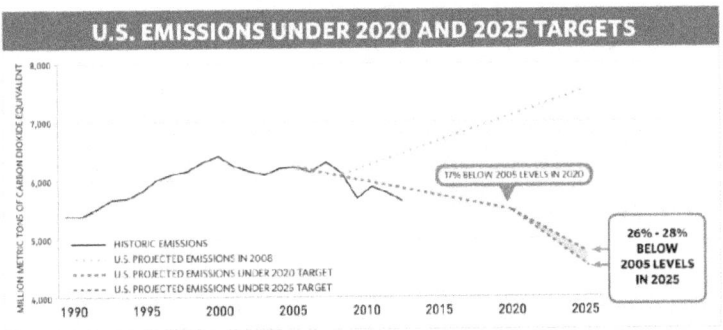

Source: UNFCCC[125]

The key to all of these commitments is that they are "country driven," meaning that each member party must carry out its commitment with its own policies. This was to become a point of contention in negotiations. India, for example, supported the concept of country-driven contributions but other parties questioned how that could be monitored.[126] The lead U.S. negotiator, Todd Stern, has lauded the INDCs because member parties "subject what they are proposing to do to full sunlight, so ... other countries and civil society and the press and everybody else can look to see what China, the U.S., Europe or Japan or anybody else is proposing to do. And you take whatever criticism you get."[127] In other words, the U.S., India and others tended to place the responsibility for implementation of the Paris Agreement at the country level, rather than at the international level.

Negotiations in Peru at COP20 (December 1-14, 2014) were preceded by a flurry of activity in the UN, including a "Climate Summit" in New York in September. Preceding the summit was a march in New York City of about 400,000 people, including participation by top leaders such as UN Secretary-General Ban Ki Moon.

Regarding Lima, Christiana Figueres, Executive Secretary of UNFCCC, said in an editorial:

> There is certainly a positive tone in the air as we come to Lima, not least as a result of the UN Secretary-General's Climate Summit in September and the events surrounding Climate Week. The presence of hundreds of thousands of citizens on the streets of New York and cities around the globe sent a clear and unequivocal signal to leaders that the public is behind climate action.[128]

While the UNFCCC bureaucracy may have a positive view of the possibilities in Lima, member parties vary in their views. Discussion in this section will focus on the BASIC countries, Brazil, South Africa, India and China, as well as the U.S., Japan and Europe.

South Africa has a rosy view of its own efforts to address climate change. According to President Jacob Zuma, "To assist all sectors to contribute to the fight against climate change, we have released the National Strategy for Sustainable Development, which is accompanied by strategies such as the new growth path and the Green Economy Strategy.... Our economy will be resilient to the possible effects of climate change only when we take bold steps, like the reduction of emission of carbon dioxide and other gases that lead to increasing global temperatures. The Department of Environmental Affairs is literally walking the green talk."[129]

Prime Minister Shinzo Abe of Japan faces a major challenge in dealing with energy demand in the wake of the Fukushima disaster. He referred to technology in addressing the challenge of climate change: "Energy will also be a key to growth. We will put an end to the regional monopolies in electricity that have been in place for 60 years and create a fee and dynamic energy market where innovation blooms. As a front-runner in the energy revolution, Japan will also make active contributions through leading-edge technologies, including the world's first commercialization of fuel cell vehicles as well as smart communities. I believe that promoting collaboration with overseas entities will be the key for further innovation." [130] Japan did not maintain its leadership position domestically, however. With the closure of most of its nuclear plants in the wake of the Fukushima disaster, it reverted to fossil fuel generation for power.[131]

President Barack Obama outlined a number of steps the U.S. has taken to reduce emissions and said, "I call on all countries to join us – not next year or the year after, but right now, because no nation can meet this global threat alone."[132] The U.S. has taken steps to reduce pollution from vehicles and power plants, but it is doubtful that the U.S. will agree to legally binding commitments. Todd Stern, the head of the U.S. delegation, said, "Many countries, including major ones, won't be willing to make their mitigation commitment legally binding at the international level, and once some balk, the premise of a legal form applicable to all unravels. Second, many countries, if forced to put forward a legally binding commitment, might low-ball that commitment out of anxiety about what legally binding might mean in this context."[133] The EU head of delegation reacted negatively to this approach: "We don't want to get to Paris and realise that the targets and the contributions did not add up to what we needed." She said that the EU wanted the 2015 agreement to have "legal force through robust rules, procedures and institutions, to ensure long-term certainty and accountability." [134] Her sentiments were reinforced by French President Hollande, who said "if the agreement is not legally binding, there is no agreement."[135]

Some officials have resisted the concept of legally binding commitments because they tend to stymie the negotiations. South African environment minister Valli Moosa said "The biggest consideration here has been what is it that will make countries put forward ambitious plans. It's very clear to everybody that the tighter the

41

legal requirements, the less ambitious will be the plans."[136] The term "ambitious" refers to the level of commitment, e.g. the U.S. commitment to reduce emissions 26-28% by 2025. Without ambitious plans, the agreement would not meet the established goal of limiting temperature rise to 2C, but without legally binding commitments parties are concerned that other parties would "free ride."[137]

The issue of legally binding commitments is one that would plague the negotiations throughout the process. The U.S. is unwilling to make legal commitments because the Obama administration would be unable to get them ratified in Congress. The EU and other parties, however, want the commitments to ensure that the emissions reductions are actually carried out. Many are concerned that, after the Obama administration leaves office, U.S. commitments may not be fulfilled. Their concern is justified, as the following op-ed in the *Wall Street Journal* indicates:

> ...the fate of the current attempt to agree on a global climate pact won't be decided around the negotiating tables in Paris a year from now, but by American voters in November 2016. President Obama has all but guaranteed that where candidates stand on implementing a Paris climate accord will be a campaign issue. As the president pointed out in the context of immigration reform, "the very nature of an executive action means that a future president could reverse those actions." A vote in the Senate to ratify a treaty would settle the issue. And by avoiding the Senate and leaving the issue open, President Obama will be forcing his fellow Democrats to defend his energy policies through the next election. They will have a lot to defend.[138]

Of course, many of the commitments that the U.S. has already made would be started before 2016. The auto industry has already agreed to double mileage by 2025 and many car models do have higher mileage now. The EPA rules on coal-fired power plants are in final stages of implementation and most utilities are phasing out coal plants. Nevertheless, other UNFCCC member parties are concerned that these rules could be overturned or modified to slow the rate of U.S. emissions reductions. Political pressures to modify the rules mount as the rules take effect, and denial ideology plays a part in weakening their implementation.

The reasoning of some skeptical governments is based on the presumption that the U.S. will not accept legally binding commitments, and therefore the other parties will see the U.S. as recalcitrant, getting them off the hook. The Australian government's expert adviser on climate policy, Professor Ross Garnaut, said "A comprehensive legally binding agreement is not possible because that is not what the US does. It is rare for the US to bind itself on anything....President Obama has made it clear that he will not support US participation in a legally binding agreement, and that instead the US has made a serious domestic commitment to implementing the ambitious objectives embodied in the Xi-Obama Agreement. China will not enter a legally binding agreement if the US does not."[139] Chinese negotiator Su Wei stated that the purpose of the Paris Agreement is to "reinforce and enhance" the 1992 convention, not rewrite it.[140] Although unstated, this suggests that China agrees with the U.S. that the 1992 agreement already authorizes commitments to emissions reductions, and there would be no need to ratify a new agreement or protocol in Congress.

As this illustrates, resistance to U.S. commitments by the U.S. Congress and its denial associates is feeding into the international negotiations in a negative way. As the U.S. debates its role in making commitments to a climate agreement, other member parties are paying close attention to the U.S. domestic political situation.

CBDR and INDC

CBDR (common but differentiated responsibilities), built into the UNFCCC agreement and the Kyoto Protocol, [141] became in issue in the Lima negotiations. Developing countries that are rapidly industrializing, including India, called for reference to CBDR to be incorporated in the new agreement.

CBDR has a long history in the negotiations for both the original UNFCCC agreement and current negotiations. Much of that history involves different views of obligations under the agreement. According to Chasek *et.al,* "North-South economic issues are a crucial element of the political context of global environmental politics. In spite of the growth of many emerging economies, including China, Brazil, India, and South Africa, to name a few, many developing countries still perceive global economic relations as fundamentally inequitable. This often shapes their policy responses to global environmental issues and their negotiating strategies on subjects as different as elephants and climate."[142] Negotiations throughout the 23 history of the UNFCCC have been mired in debates over the relative responsibilities of different member parties. "Developing countries continue to insist that the industrialized countries, because of their historical dominance in the … combustion of fossil fuels are responsible for environmental problems and should bear the responsibility for any solution. More generally, they identify the high levels of consumption in industrialized countries as a key cause of global environmental degradation."[143] Consumption is an issue that we will return to in Chapter 7.

It is indeed because of this history that the UNFCCC was adopted with provisions for "different responsibilities" to right the inequalities of global economic relations. The "common but differentiated responsibilities" provisions have also created much of the opposition in some countries, notably the U.S., that have fed into resistance by denial ideologues.

When negotiations led some to believe that the agreement would downplay these provisions, developing countries in the Group of 77, known as G-77, objected. "This whole exercise is not meant to rewrite the convention, this is a firm basic position of the G-77. We stand behind the differentiation, we stand behind 'common but differentiated responsibilities', these are issues we hold very strong and these are definite red lines," said Antonio Marcondes, Brazil's representative at the talks. [144] Brazil also proposed using a concept of "concentric circles," with industrialized countries at the center, emerging economies the next circle out from the center, and least developed countries further out. Each circle would have different responsibilities. This concept was not incorporated into the Paris Agreement, however.

Brazil has a domestic problem that may affect its international negotiating position. Its science minister, Aldo Rebelo, has expressed denial of climate science: "The positivist scientism that you call natural science and contrast with my devotion to dialectical materialism is not magical enough to convert me to the article of faith that is the theory of global warming, which is incompatible with current knowledge. Science is not an oracle. In fact, *there is no scientific proof of the projections of global warming,* much less that it is occurring because of human action and not because of natural phenomena. It is a construct based on computer simulations."[145] Rebelo is a communist, and Marxism has been associated with a Promethean view of nature that tends toward a perspective that humans can overcome any natural limits. [146] Perhaps he would prefer that Brazil not participate in negotiations at all, but he would likely be overruled by President Dilma Rousseff.

China and India insisted on including the phrase "in light of different national circumstances" in the text, to carve out a provision for economic development in the context of reducing emissions.[147] This phrase makes the "nationally determined" part of Intended Nationally Determined Contributions (INDCs, below) a point of disparity in commitments. When two of the highest emitters reserve the right to pollute more than other high-emission parties, the success of the agreement is in jeopardy.

Developed countries such as Japan, the U.S., and Australia opposed creating divisions on commitments or the distinction between developed and developing countries.[148] These members are listed in Annex I of the UNFCCC, and negotiations could hinge on retaining or discarding Annex I. The U.S. called for an option in the text to update the Convention's annexes to reflect parties' changing economic and emissions trends, a clear reference to India, Brazil and China.[149] This change was resisted by the developing countries, however. The rift would plague the negotiations throughout the year between Lima and Paris (see Chapter 4). "This issue will be contentious and it will need to be worked through all the way to Paris," said U.S. climate envoy Todd Stern.[150]

One reason that CBDR is so contentious is that denial ideologues make it into one of the main arguments against negotiation of an effective agreement. Some go so far as to argue that CBDR is the main impetus for the original UNFCCC agreement. Recounting the time when the UNFCCC was under negotiation in the early 1990s, Larry Bell makes the following analysis.

> This was also a time when Third World countries, by force of numbers, and European socialist green parties, through powers of aggressiveness, seized control of the United Nations to advance globalization goals, which emerging global warming alarm perfectly served. Accordingly, the United Nations established the Framework Convention on Climate Change (UN-FCCC) to organize conferences, along with the UN's IPCC which, prior to any studies, concluded that climate change caused by fossil burning posed a global threat.[151]

46

Of course, Bell does not believe that "climate change caused by fossil burning posed a global threat." He regards climate science as invalid, and suggests that the parties negotiating the agreement are "advancing globalization goals" through "seizing control of the United Nations. In other words, they are using climate science as a subterfuge to take over the world. This kind of analysis is typical of denial ideology, attributing nefarious motives to those who use climate science as a rationale for negotiating climate agreements.[152]

Ultimately, the issue of CBDR comes down to: will all of the countries in the world participate in reducing emissions to the extent required to keep temperature increases below 2C? Some, such as India, believe that developed countries must "yield" some space in the atmosphere to developing countries. "Today, I see the carbon space occupied by the developed world. We are asking the developed world to vacate the carbon space to accommodate us. That carbon space demand is climate justice," according to Prakash Javadekar, the environment minister.[153] This is a contentious issue because it poses obligations to national development against obligations to international accountability for climate change. Welzer argues "The climate change debate is full of such traps. [An] example is whether societies behind in modernization should be allowed the same pollution rights that early industrialized countries had in an age when no one gave a thought to such matters. In the present day, when the consequences of a heedless attitude are known, a question like that expresses nothing other than a kind of forced stupidity."[154]

"Forced stupidity" is a rather crude way of saying that all parties to climate change agreements must recognize that, with knowledge from scientific research, none can sensibly avoid the implications of "heedless" development. Negotiations of the Paris Agreement had to build on this recognition to be successful in addressing climate change. While parties vary in the pace at which

they reduce emissions, none can abjure their obligations to do so.

Intended Nationally Determined Contributions (INDC) are one of the major issues of the negotiations. INDCs are pledges of carbon emissions reductions that would collectively be designed to reduce CO2 and other greenhouse gases to a level to avoid "dangerous human influence on the climate." That level has been determined by agreement to be 2 degrees Celsius or less, but the pledges made in the run-up to the Paris meeting will "not get us onto the 2C pathway," according to UNFCCC Executive Secretary Christiana Figueres. [155] She has finessed the issue by saying "This question now is one of speed and scale. It is not a question of whether we will get to 2 degrees."[156]

While most parties agree that INDC's are a necessary indicator of progress toward keeping global temperatures below a 2C increase, there is disagreement on how to measure and report them. Brazil has resisted the concept of legally binding obligations in reporting INDCs. South Africa, Japan and China have supported international communication of INDC levels so that other parties can assess them. Interestingly, Russia has opposed this level of transparency.[157] China and India do not want to go beyond subjecting INDC levels to a modicum of international review and assessment, implying that such reporting may not be used for enforcement.

Another INDC issue is timing. The U.S. has proposed that the INDCs have a target date of 2025 (a date used by President Obama in the agreement with China – see Chapter 1). Japan has requested that the timing be stretched out to 2030, perhaps because it has encountered difficulties in replacing nuclear energy. In its submission, Japan justified the longer time frame "because a longer-term target will send a long-term signal to investors, and because it enables us to set a more ambitious target, which takes into account the impact of drastic measures which redirect investment activities of domestic actors."[158] Translation: we need time to reorient our energy system.

In addition to the target date for the goals, there was also debate over how quickly member parties should submit their INDCs for review by other members. The U.S., for example, wanted to have INDCs ready for review by April 1, 2015 while developing country members want more time. Brazil and South Africa wanted to extend the deadline to June 30.[159] While this may seem like quibbling, the issue of review is contentious and demonstrates different views of how data will affect decisions. It also affects the nature of the intersessional meetings (see Chapter 4) that must adjust the text of the proposed agreement based on how the parties frame their INDCs.

In Peru, the final decision on submission of timing was a compromise. While encouraging member parties to submit INDCs by April 1, 2015, the delegates decided to allow a three-month "grace period" for submission by June 30. There is no enforcement mechanism to insure that the submissions are timely or comparable. China and some developing countries blocked a proposal for a review process that would allow the commitments to be compared against each other. Instead, the UNFCCC secretariat drafted a report analyzing the "aggregate" effect of all pledges a month before the COP in Paris.

Brazil raised another issue about INDCs. "We favor a transparent presentation of country issues, but we think that an ex-ante review [in 2015] would be an unnecessary effort," said Minister Marcondes. "It would detract from the main goal of reaching Paris with a new agreement."[160] In other words, if developing countries submit weak commitments and the developed countries judge them as inadequate, chances for an agreement in Paris would be reduced. Weak commitments might be opportunities for other parties to reduce their own "ambitions." The text agreed in Peru did allow for "special circumstances" of least developed countries,

49

however. Presumably their commitments would be conditioned on their need for development.

There is also disagreement over the base year for measuring emissions reductions when reporting INDCs. The U.S., for example, has been using 2005 as a base year while the EU prefers 1990, the year built into the original UNFCCC agreement and the Kyoto Protocol. Japan is neutral on the matter but does insist on including base years in the INDC reporting, which would otherwise be useless for comparison of levels of ambition.

"Ambition" is in fact a term that is often used in the negotiations, because many developing countries want the industrialized world to be more ambitious in reducing emissions. China, for example, said, "information on INDCs should enhance clarity of developed countries' ambition."[161] Translation: industrialized countries should do more to mitigate climate change. China itself has resisted monitoring of its emissions, even as it has agreed to cap them.[162] India is also resistant to the idea of outside evaluation of its commitments on emissions. [163] Nevertheless, the text agreed in Peru was a step toward enhancing action on emissions.

Because of built-in inertia, the climate system is now responding to emissions accumulated over the past 250 years and will continue to change in the future regardless of how much emissions are reduced. The original text of the UNFCCC convention reads, in Article 2 (Objective), "The ultimate objective of this Convention and any related legal instruments that the Conference of the Parties may adopt is to achieve, in accordance with the relevant provisions of the Convention, stabilization of greenhouse gas concentrations in the atmosphere at a level that would prevent dangerous anthropogenic interference with the climate system." [164] The term *"prevent"* is problematic to the parties, as they cannot predict what would prevent "dangerous interference" and some believe that dangerous interference is already built in. This has led one expert to conclude, "The talks are well past the stage of attempting to avoid climate change;

instead, they are effectively focused on preventing things from turning from bad to devastating. In 2010, the countries participating in the U.N. climate process set a goal to keep the global temperature rise below 2 degrees Celsius (3.6 degrees Fahrenheit) above pre-industrial levels. Exceeding that, they agreed, would expose the planet – not to mention humankind – to potential catastrophe. Some actually argue that 2 degrees is too high. The problem is that we're already almost there.[165] The analysis that we are beyond "preventing" dangerous human interference with the climate and that we are now in the process of *"preventing things from turning from bad to devastating"* is a discouraging prospect. Some in the denial community would use this argument to assert that further action is futile.

One of the *"devastating"* aspects of climate change is extreme weather, and delegates from the Philippines have prodded the negotiators to do more. In 2013 Typhoon Haiyan struck the Philippines during COP-19 and in 2014 Typhoon Hagupit hit during COP-20. Philippines delegates mentioned these storms as evidence of climate change (though some have questioned that[166]), and called for more ambitious action on mitigation as well as enhanced financing for adaptation.[167]

In the last stages of negotiation of INDCs – timing and review – the text was weakened by making the deadlines and assessment lax and late in the process. A summary report on Lima concluded, "Considered by some the weakest link of the Lima outcome, the decision text simply requests that the Secretariat publish the communicated INDCs on the UNFCCC website and prepare, by 1 November 2015, a synthesis report on their aggregate effect. This translates into an absence of any kind of *ex ante* review of individual contributions in 2015. Further, it also leaves parties with less than a month for possible upward adjustment prior to COP 21 in Paris in December 2015."[168]

When the INDCs were tallied in late October 2015, they did fall somewhat short. UN's climate chief,

Christiana Figueres said "The INDCs have the capability of limiting the forecast temperature rise to around 2.7C by 2100, by no means enough but a lot lower than the estimated four, five, or more degrees of warming projected by many prior to the INDCs."[169] This somewhat successful outcome indicates that Lima did have a positive effect on member parties' commitments.

The final outcome in Lima was somewhat vague and showed the ambivalence of the negotiators. "In the end, the Lima decision largely sidestepped the issue, which is certain to be a central challenge in reaching an agreement in Paris."[170] The *Lima Call for Climate Action* may have one unintended positive outcome, however. Because debate has shifted from what member parties should do to how they do it, the tenor of the talks may become more technical and less political. "Paris could be an opportunity to change that, if it identifies the cornerstones of the work that needs to be done. It could make it into a technical process and not a political process," according to Yvo de Boer, a former U.N. climate chief and head of the Global Green Growth Institute. [171] As member parties begin the process of reviewing each other's commitments, they may coalesce around practical steps to resolve climate change.

Financing

Financing, one of the major issues in planning for the Paris Agreement, became touchy during the Lima negotiations. Financing is an issue both for mitigation (reducing emissions) and adaptation to climate change. Even more wealthy developing countries are expected to support financing in less developed countries. China and India have both been asked to do more with financing "green growth" in the least developed countries. "Green growth" is a concept that developing countries could leapfrog energy infrastructure growth by adopting renewable energies in place of fossil-fueled energy.

China and India favor more financing of green growth but do not want their contributions to displace contributions to the Global Climate Fund promised by developed countries.[172] They have objected to language in the proposed text that calls for "parties [to] mobilize and provide financial resources in a manner which is capable of adapting dynamically to changing realities and future developments and needs." [173] Translation: as their economies grow, China and India are expected to provide more financing.

China and India also suggested mobilization and provision of finance be enhanced not "in coordination with," but rather as "additional to," official development assistance. [174] This is a call for additional financing outside of the usual aid programs. Japan and the EU are also concerned about financing green growth, but from a developed country perspective. They have objected to the term "upscaling," when that implies higher rates of future contributions. [175] Japan has also indicated that it is concerned about the need for developing countries to improve their investment environments.[176] If developed countries or businesses want to finance green growth, the conditions must be favorable for decent returns on investments.

A perennial problem of financing is the amount provided by rich countries to help out with mitigating and adapting to climate change in poorer countries. In Copenhagen rich countries pledged up to $100 billion a year by 2020, but in 2014 only $10 was fully committed. "We are disappointed. It is ridiculous. It is ridiculously low," said Minister for Environment, Forest & Climate Change Prakash Javadekar of India. [177] There is some dispute about this number, however, as the OECD has countered with analysis that shows $62 billion in climate financing in 2014. Developing country leaders dislike the OECD accounting because it includes loans and private financing.

Financing is not just a practical matter of providing resources for mitigating or adapting to climate change. It also has an economic justice connotation. "If countries are not required to make legal contributions on finance and technology there will be no justice – and if there's no justice there cannot be a deal," according to Lidy Nacpil of Jubilee South Asia Pacific from the Philippines. [178] This aspect of financing sets up the conditions for conflict between developed countries that provide the financing and developing countries that blame the industrialized world for creating the problem.[179]

One phrase in the text, "loss and damage," has become a point of contention. Originally proposed in Warsaw at COP19 (2013), the concept of "loss and damage" – commonly interpreted as meaning "liability and compensation" – raised the possibility of further financial obligations of developed countries, putting them at loggerheads with developing countries such as the small islands whose very existence is threatened by rising sea levels.[180] AOSIS (Association of Small Island States) has pushed for more ambitious financial commitments, i.e. a limit of 1.5C rather than 2C, seeking to avoid the inundation of their homelands from sea level rise.

In the end, delegates in Lima disagreed over whether the text should refer to "loss and damage."[181] This issue is one that would plague negotiations on the Paris Agreement, as it suggests that industrialized countries are responsible for the increasing costs of adaptation in developing countries. While a moral argument can be made for this assignment of responsibility, it is problematic from a legal perspective and delegations from the U.S. and Japan, for example, tend to shy away from such language.

Loss and damage is an area of international negotiations that has attracted the attention of denial ideologues. Carlin argues that, if fully implemented, loss and damage provisions could cost developed countries "trillions of dollars."

> Instead of taking measures to reduce the adverse effects of these weather events, they are demanding a new UN agency to calculate and distribute loss and damage benefits using large additional

payments from the developed world, and this was agreed to (with US and other developed nations' approval) at the 2013 UN Warsaw COP Conference as a new UN legal framework, the Warsaw International Mechanism for Loss and Damage Associated with Climate Change Impacts. And instead of making the scientifically supportable viewpoint that there is no scientific basis for [global warming], the US and other developed countries are left arguing when and how much their payments should be. Such payments for weather damages could well cost many trillions of dollars if the developed world should ever agree to actually pay them.[182]

Carlin's analysis begs the question, what is the cost of climate change if reductions are not curtailed? The UN Office for Disaster Risk Reduction, based in Geneva, has estimated that climate change has already cost $1.9 trillion. Based on analysis by the Center for Research on the Epidemiology of Disasters, based in Belgium, the figure of $1.9 trillion is likely to rise in future years and far outstrip the "trillions of dollars" mentioned by Carlin. More significantly, extreme weather related to climate change has already killed 600,000 people.[183]

Finance issues have drawn the interest of denial proponents. Senator Mike Lee (R-UT) introduced a resolution in the U.S. Senate. It specifically mentioned the Green Climate Fund: "Congress should refuse to consider any budget resolutions and appropriations language that include funding for the Green Climate Fund or any affiliated body or financial mechanism unless and until all agreements on emissions targets and timetables are submitted to the Senate for advice and consent."[184] Lee was trying to make U.S. contributions to the fund contingent on submission of the Paris Agreement to the Senate, which was unlikely to approve the agreement.

The Obama administration made every effort to avoid this possibility.

Sabotaging the Agreement?

Agreeing on emissions reductions is no longer just a matter of responding to the science. It has become a moral issue. "Future generations will judge our effort not just as a policy failure, but as a massive, collective moral failure of historic consequence, particularly if we're just bogged down in abstract debates," according to U.S. Secretary of State John Kerry.[185] *"Abstract debates"* are becoming frequent and detracting more and more from the main issues of climate change: the use of fossil fuel energy and its role in modern economies. Kerry also chided delegates about focusing on CBDR issues: "we have to remember that today more than half of emissions are coming from developing nations, so it is imperative that they act, too."[186]

Brazil, for example, has criticized developed countries for their weak commitments on INDCs and financing. Yet Brazil itself is rushing headlong to develop fossil fuels and coal-fired electricity. "Brazil is going full speed with investments in areas off its coast that could hold up to 35 billion barrels of oil. Scrambling for energy as a severe drought depletes hydro power plants' reservoirs, the country has just approved new coal-fired plants that would be partially financed by the government."[187] The ironic juxtaposition of increasing emissions that cause the drought, while complaining about worldwide emissions and financing, is striking.

Whether the INDCs committed by member parties in 2015 are followed in subsequent years is another question mark hovering over the negotiations. One observer of past commitments notes, "Leaders at home and abroad have consistently made pledges and committed to policy only to pivot away later as costs were revealed. Pledge and backslide seems to be the dominant climate policy trend of the last 20 years, with no government immune. Examples include the weakening of the European Union emission trading system, the inability of the U.S. to implement policy consistent with its 2009 targets until very recently, Canada's eight national climate change plans, and Australia's long and winding road in and out of carbon pricing. Even Germany, that hotbed of green energy, is of late burning more coal, putting its GHG targets at risk." [188] This catalog of policies adopted and then weakened shows that even with fairly firm and realistic commitments, member parties have not been consistent in carrying out their obligations.[189]

Pope Francis, visiting Tacloban in the Philippines to review the damage from Typhoon Haiyan, called for more courage than displayed in the Lima negotiations. "The Peru meeting was nothing much, it disappointed me. I think there was a lack of courage. They stopped at a certain point. Let's hope the delegates in Paris will be more courageous and move forward with this." [190] The pope did seem more positive when he addressed the UN General Assembly in September 2015: "I am ... confident that the Paris Conference on Climatic Change will secure fundamental and effective agreements."[191]

Pope Francis' efforts to address climate change with his encyclical *Laudato Si* (see Chapter 4) have elicited a negative response from one denial organization, Cornwall Alliance:

> What the Pope fails to realize is that **the Green movement is intrinsically anti-human, anti-children, and anti-future generations!** The Green movement will use this summit and its resulting statement to push the Paris Climate Agreement through in December. **We cannot stand by and let that happen.** The Cornwall Alliance and Pope Francis share many common values that the Green movement opposes. As people who share the Pope's Biblical worldview and the ethic of godly human dominion over the

57

earth, we are in a unique position to reach out to Pope Francis and explain to him why regulations meant to fight global warming will harm people everywhere – the poor, of whom the Pope has been a champion for many decades, most of all.[192]

Cornwall Alliance demonstrates two of the tenets of denial ideology, the assertion that humans have "dominion over the earth" and that fighting global warming will harm the poor most of all. Of course, these tenets ignore the dependence of humans on ecological services and the probabilities that climate change will harm the poor more than any likely climate actions.[193] Exploitation of fossil fuels for development, particularly in poor regions of the world, is much more likely to hurt the poor than development of alternative forms of energy. Of course, if fossil fuels are not fully utilized, some will have to be left in the ground. That may hurt wealthy oil companies much more than the poor.[194]

When the pope visited Washington, DC in September 2015, Cornwall Alliance unloaded another broadside against climate science.

Pope Francis, President Obama, and many others believe anthropogenic (manmade) global warming is so dangerous that the peoples of the world should spend literally trillions of dollars trying to prevent it by reducing emissions of carbon dioxide (CO2), which would require tremendous reductions in the use of fossil fuels (coal, oil, and natural gas) for electricity and vehicle fuels. There are two problems with this.

1. The first is that the claim of dangerous manmade warming is almost certainly false... there is little or nothing to fear about the slight warming our CO2 emissions might cause, and little or no justification for any policy to reduce CO2 emission – especially one costing trillions of

dollars that could be better spent solving more urgent problems.

2. The second, which we'll mention only briefly, is that spending all that money on mitigating climate change means not spending it on much more urgent problems like access to pure drinking water, sewage sanitation, adequate nutrition, communicable diseases, air and water and solid waste pollution, and access to electricity, all of which are of greatest concern to the world's poor today.[195]

When Cornwall Alliance claims that *"there is little or nothing to fear about the slight warming our CO2 emissions might cause,"* one wonders what pseudoscience they are using. Having dismissed valid climate science, Cornwall Alliance then goes on to argue that money should be spent on water, sewage, etc. for the benefit of the "world's poor."

Cornwall Alliance is influential with members of Congress, and at least one echoed its message. "At this pivotal moment in world history, His Holiness, Pope Francis, is intending to spend the majority of his time on one of the world's greatest stages focusing on climate change. If the Pope plans to spend the majority of his time advocating for flawed climate-change policies, then I will not attend," said Paul Gosar (R-AZ). Representative Gosar boycotted the Pope's address to a joint session of Congress on September 24, 2015. Most members of Congress listened politely but only a few (about 4% of Republican House members) showed much enthusiasm about the Pope's call for supporting a Paris Agreement.[196]

Other denial ideologues have addressed the prospects for international cooperation more directly. Some, such as Alan Carlin, regard the negotiations as cynical efforts by developing countries to get the U.S. and other developed countries to reduce their emissions.

Further reductions in US CO2 emissions will not reduce global temperatures in any measureable way, so

59

presumably they plan to use these controls as bargaining chips to get less developed nations to reduce their emissions. The history of recent UN climate meetings, however, shows that the less developed countries will at most offer vague, unenforceable emission reductions in return for US promises of reductions through EPA regulations... And less developed countries appear to have no interest in cutting emissions themselves in the near term, particularly without firm guarantees of the annual $100 billion in developed country support promised at Copenhagen... If there is a new international agreement, it is highly likely to be so watered down as to be meaningless. And for this the Obama Administration proposes to impose real costs on the US economy and population. [197]

In this view, it seems that anything the U.S. does is futile, because other countries would simply take advantage of our naivety and offer meaningless proposals. This kind of denial ideology appeals to politicians who do not want to do anything about climate change, since it gives them an opportunity to deny funding for finance under the Paris Agreement (see Chapter 5).

An issue that is not explicitly included in the negotiations is the issue of "stranded assets." [198] Fossil fuel companies are likely to have oil and coal reserves that cannot be burned if the goals set by the negotiations are implemented. "ExxonMobil and Shell would cease to exist in their current forms in 35 years under measures UN negotiators are considering for a legally binding global climate pact to be sealed in Paris. The oil and gas these companies produce, and the coal mined by groups such as Rio Tinto, would have to be phased out by 2050 in one proposal at UN climate talks in Lima this week, which aim to smooth a path to the Paris deal." [199] Scientists have estimated that 80% of identified reserves must stay in the ground if UN goals are to be met, but fossil fuel companies, with the support of subsidies,[200] continue to invest billions of dollars in developing new reserves. Politicians in the U.S. and other countries insist on continuing growth in fossil fuel development, railing against a "war on coal" when regulations crimp the extraction of fossil fuels.[201]

How would the issue of stranded assets affect negotiations? George Monbiot of the *Guardian* suggests that the negotiators must include a provision that would limit exploration for, and exploitation of, fossil fuel reserves:

> Scientific assessments of the carbon contained in existing fossil fuel reserves suggest that full exploitation of these reserves is incompatible with the agreed target of no more than 2C of global warming. The unrestricted extraction of these reserves undermines attempts to limit greenhouse gas emissions. We will start negotiating a global budget for the extraction of fossil fuels from existing reserves, as well as a date for a moratorium on the exploration and development of new reserves. In line with the quantification of the fossil carbon that can be extracted without a high chance of exceeding 2C of global warming, we will develop a timetable for annual reductions towards that budget. We will develop mechanisms for allocating production within this budget and for enforcement and monitoring.[202]

Such a provision would fly in the face of the current mode of development and use of fossil fuels. It would require a major overhaul of energy systems throughout the world, a change that many scientists regard as necessary to avoid the worst consequences of climate change. Could negotiators manage to agree on a provision such as this? It is highly unlikely, given the intense level of opposition it would arouse in the societies of member parties, particularly the developed economies.

Greenpeace UK executive director John Sauven made a trenchant observation about how the potential for stranded assets will focus denial opposition to the Paris Agreement.

> The climate denial lobby and its fossil fuel funders will be even more focused in the coming months. For us this might just be the end of the beginning. For them it's the beginning of the end. Once the world starts setting hard limits on emissions, all the business plans of all the oil majors in the world become obsolete, wishful thinking and the global economy starts adjusting to a low-carbon future in earnest. From that day forward fossil fuels go into permanent retreat. So expect to see a frenzied last-ditch defence of the fossil fuel economy, with climate science under greater attack than ever before. With trillions of dollars at stake, don't expect a clean fight.[203]

Using Churchillian language, Sauven views negotiations in Lima and Paris as "the end of the beginning," but for fossil fuel companies and their denial defenders it is *the beginning of the end.*" If the Paris Agreement does succeed in reducing emissions, it will significantly reduce the value of their assets.

Fossil fuel companies seem to be counting on the likelihood that negotiations of a Paris Agreement will not affect the value of their reserves.

> But at present, hydrocarbon valuations in the world market seem to be operating on the assumption that climate policies will be very weak and medium-term carbon prices close to zero, which is a stance also,

apparently, shared by the world's largest publicly traded oil and gas company, ExxonMobil. Essentially they are arguing that while their valuations of their assets would be contradicted by sensible climate policies, they are banking on the failure of good sense on the climate front.[204]

If climate policies are "weak," and carbon prices are zero, the effectiveness of the national governments who commit themselves through INDCs (see Chapter 3) is called into question. In that case, the Paris Agreement will not be effective.

UN's climate chief, Christiana Figueres also made the point that stranded assets would reduce the value of fossil fuel companies. "Those corporations that continue to invest in new fossil fuel exploration, new fossil fuel exploitation, are really in flagrant breach of their fiduciary duty because the science is abundantly clear that this is something we can no longer do."[205] *Flagrant breach of fiduciary duty* is a serous charge, but if one looks at the amount of fossil fuel reserves already identified, it appears that there may be five times as much available as can be burned. Further exploration would indeed seem to be flagrant breach of responsibility to shareholders, but fossil fuel companies continue to spend hundreds of billions on exploration. Apparently they are not concerned about the possibility that their assets would be compromised by an effective Paris Agreement.

Resistance to commitments in the Paris Agreement may not come directly from the fossil fuel companies, but their political allies will sabotage the agreement whenever possible. Whether the sabotage is in the form of denying the science or simply trying to avoid support for implementing the agreement depends on the politicians. They do have plenty of support, not only in the business community, but also among the population, when they capitalize on denial tendencies.[206] Some politicians such as Senator Inhofe will continue to

63

sabotage climate action regardless of what negotiators agreed on.

It does not take long for the denial ideologues to find reasons to sabotage the agreement. Here's a catalogue of gripes from the American Enterprise Institute (AEI): "Will China and India and the other major underdeveloped emitters of greenhouse gases commit economic suicide so as to satisfy the demands of the environmental left? Will the major developed nations commit economic suicide by shifting toward fantastically expensive energy and by imposing even higher taxes upon themselves so as to achieve a deal? Will the U.S-China romance last? Will the climate industry achieve its dreams? Or will we someday read about the 100th COP? *No, no, no, no and yes*."[207]

Apparently, the greatest sin of climate negotiators is to continue meeting (*the 100th COP, i.e. 2095*) while nations such as China and India refuse to meet the demands of the *"environmental left"* and developed nations refuse to *"impose even higher taxes on themselves to achieve a deal."* While AEI may have a point about member parties refusing to make real efforts, the agreement itself will not take until 2095 to come to fruition. Well before then emissions will fall, either gradually from real efforts to reduce them or drastically from economic collapse.

While most denial groups stayed home during the negotiations, at least one showed up.

This year, when the Committee for a Constructive Tomorrow (CFACT) – a well-oiled, highly funded fossil fuel stink tank – showed up, barely anyone engaged. Only two journalists were at their press conference, and one of them was even caught on tape making the outrageous claim that "delegates from poor nations are showing up to the international climate accords just so they collect a per diem and take a vacation with their families." And so the climate deniers were a bit of freakshow this

64

time around in Lima and garnered only negative attention. We just need to be careful and remember that they're still out there, they're still getting paid and they're actively working on their next attack.[208]

Apparently the UNFCCC principle of common but differentiated responsibilities (CBDR) is offensive to CFACT. They regard *"delegates from poor nations"* as freeloaders, taking advantage of support for their attendance. These delegates have a legitimate role in advancing the interests of their governments. CBDR does recognize the fact that most developing countries have had little deleterious effect on the climate and may need some support in pursuit of low-carbon development.

Regarding CBDR, some denial ideologues have turned the idea of differentiation of responsibilities against the whole agreement. In a sarcastic statement, *Cornwall Alliance* castigates member parties for agreeing on the necessity for emissions reductions:

> Reductions in carbon dioxide emissions will damage developing nations the worst – creating higher energy prices for people already too poor to barely feed themselves. Western countries are taking the blame for the current "catastrophe" (remember there has been no global warming in 18 years), because they used fossil fuels to rise out of poverty. Developing nations have to follow that path as well, if they want to pull their populations out of the cycle of hunger, disease, and death. So why are the developing nations even coming to the table? Bribery. Guilt money to be exact. The Western countries are giving money to developing nations to "mitigate" the effects of climate change. Climate change for which we (the West) apparently hold the blame. Yes, let's blame us for using fossil fuels, let's blame us for eradicating many diseases, for

65

increased food production, for lifting millions out of poverty (and attempting to lift millions more), for thousands of advanced technologies that have benefited mankind, and the environment.[209]

Cornwall Alliance uses a number of canards to justify its rant against the agreement. The canard about the globe cooling (*there has been no global warming in 18 years*) is followed by canards about *bribery* and *guilt money,* which presumably lead developing countries to agree to emissions reductions that are against their best interests. The canard about fossil fuels *"eradicating many diseases, increasing food production, lifting millions out of poverty"* assumes that there are no other forms of energy or agricultural practices that can accomplish these goals. *Cornwall Alliance* also conveniently ignores the probability that climate change will exacerbate poverty.[210]

What is the effect of such statements? While *Cornwall Alliance* does not have much credibility in the delegations to UNFCCC COPs, it can sway public opinion in the U.S. It counts among its luminaries scientists such as Roy Spencer of the University of Alabama and Kenneth Chilton, Ph.D., Senior Environmental Fellow, Institute for the Study of Economics & the Environment, Lindenwood University. It may influence U.S. policymakers to try to sabotage the agreement through votes in Congress.[211]

Much more subtle forms of sabotage are found throughout the negotiations. None of the delegates, for example, explicitly proposes to exceed the two-degree limit agreed in Cancun, and most give at least lip service to that criterion for success. When confronted with the actual numbers for emissions that would contain warming to that level, however, delegates shy away from hard commitments. To attain the "prevention of dangerous anthropogenic interference in the climate," however, would require rapid and significant reductions in emissions. This would, in turn, strand many of the assets discussed earlier and impose tight limits on how much fossil fuel could be extracted and used. Governments shy away from confronting the fossil fuel industry and try to finesse the commitments by referring mostly to carbon dioxide equivalents, not explicitly referring to the underlying energy production that causes the emissions.

Despite their worst efforts, however, delegates did manage to salvage the agreement at the last minute. In what is being called the "Lima Call for Climate Action," member parties agreed to make commitments of INDCs by March 31, 2015, with extensions to June 30, a compromise that was worked out by the Peruvian chairman of the COP, Environment Minister Manuel Pulgar-Vidal. In another compromise, the approved draft weakened language on the content of the pledges, saying they "may" instead of "shall" include quantifiable information showing how countries intend to meet their emissions targets.[212]

"I think it's definitely watered down from what we expected," said Alden Meyer of the Union of Concerned Scientists. [213] The CBDR issue has not been fully resolved, as some developing countries have reserved their right to differential treatment. "While all countries will be required under the Lima Call for Climate Action to submit plans to reduce emissions, the nature of the plans can be different according to the size of their economies. Rich countries, like the United States, are expected to put forward plans detailing how they would put their emissions on a downward trajectory after 2020. Large but developing economies, like China, are more likely to put forward plans that name a future year in which their emissions peak. Poorer economies are expected to put forward plans indicating that their pollution will continue to increase — but at a lower rate."[214] More ambitious commitments will be required, either in the lead-up to Paris or during negotiations there. "Much remains to be done in Paris next year," French Foreign Minister Laurent Fabius said.

Lima did give some observers reason for optimism: "the Lima agreement can be seen as a move toward a more natural form of cooperation, in which ongoing interaction, negotiation and shared growth in understanding can lead to a solution. Humanity need not be locked into a choice between disaster or global government just because some oversimplified model says so."[215] While many denial advocates have railed against "global government,"[216] the Lima Call for Climate Action sidesteps this issue by making the INDCs "nationally determined." This avoids the problem of instituting an international enforcement regime. Of course, it also makes the INDCs less stringent and throws into question the effectiveness of the UNFCCC.

One indication of the tentativeness of the negotiations in Lima was a footnote added to the COP decision on the negotiation text: "delegates agreed to…a disclaimer contained in a footnote stating that the elements for a draft negotiating text reflect work in progress and neither indicate convergence on the proposals presented, nor do they preclude new proposals from emerging in the course of negotiations in 2015."[217]

Developing countries are still hoping for more *ambitious* commitments from developed countries: "This disclaimer addressed concerns raised by many developing countries that annexing the elements text to the COP decision might preempt the legal form, structure or content of the Paris Agreement and were therefore against *formalizing* any language that could potentially exclude some options from consideration in 2015, while locking in others."[218]

An indication of the weakness of the proposed text is this set of complaints by 350.org: "The new agreement does not reflect the urgency of the climate crisis. There are some good agreements, but no measures to ensure implementation. Least developed and vulnerable nations left out in the cold. Divestment is more important than ever. Global momentum for real solutions is stronger than ever and will keep on going." Of course, 350.org is an advocacy organization and the call for divestment and "global momentum" is part of its agenda.

It does have grass-roots support among youth in many countries, so its views may have some effect. Whether negotiators will meet their expectations will depend on details to be thrashed out during the intersessional negotiations and finalized in Paris.

Chapter 4
Intersessional Negotiations and Events

Between COP 20 and COP 21, intersessional negotiations occurred Geneva in February 2015 and in Bonn – June, August/September and October 2015. Geneva, Switzerland is the home of many UN agencies and Bonn, Germany, is the home of the secretariat of UNFCCC. Bonn has hosted many intersessional meetings in past years.

Many readers might wonder why the UNFCCC needs to hold intersessional negotiations when all the member parties gather once a year for COPs. Intersessional meetings also give parties chances to negotiate some of the details of the text to be endorsed at the high-level segment of the COPs. Usually the delegates to these intersessional meetings are not authorized to sign off the text until it is reviewed by capitols for final negotiation at the COPs. Nevertheless, they can agree to edit text and streamline the agreement by combining similar items and organizing the text.

One area for intersessional review is the degree to which parties must implement commitments rapidly. UNFCCC convention text includes the "precautionary principle."

The Parties should take precautionary measures to anticipate, prevent or minimize the causes of climate change and mitigate its adverse effects. Where there are threats of serious or irreversible damage, lack of full scientific certainty should not be used as a reason for postponing such measures, taking into account that policies and measures to deal with climate change should be cost-effective so as to ensure global benefits at the lowest possible cost. To achieve this, such policies and measures should take into account different socio-economic contexts, be comprehensive, cover all relevant sources, sinks and reservoirs of greenhouse gases and adaptation, and comprise all economic sectors.

This text has been the source of problems in negotiations throughout the history of UNFCCC: "...arguments exist that it should not be accepted as a principle of international law (on par with universally accepted principles such as sovereignty)." [219] If not embodied in international law, how can the member parties enforce the agreement? Much of the discussion of implementing the INDCs in the intersessional negotiations hinged on this question.

Why has the precautionary principle become so controversial? It stems from the fact that precaution is based on scientific research while action on climate change is often based on economic factors such as cost-benefit analysis of renewable energies. The precautionary principle requires action even in the absence of scientific certainty, and there is plenty of uncertainty in climate science. Strenuous efforts are underway to reduce this uncertainty. With increasing interest in environmental issues, scientific research comes to the fore as an issue, often provoking backlash.[220]

> As environmental issues, like climate change, have become more technical, and as scientific uncertainty about possible long-term effects has grown, policy makers rely on scientists to present the facts and projections, which often set the stage for treaty negotiations. As a result, international networks of cooperating scientists and scientific institutions have become actors in global environmental policy.[221]

In the case of UNFCCC negotiations, the IPCC is the scientific institution that set the stage for negotiations.[222] IPCC assessment reports are published in advance of negotiations, as was the case in 2014. One of the sponsoring organizations of the IPCC, the World Meteorological Organization (WMO), reviews temperature records during the intersessional period and reports on years with the highest temperatures. WMO has already announced that 2014 had the highest temperatures since records were established in the 1880s.[223] During the intersessional negotiations WMO kept updating its announcements with indications that 2015 would become another record year. These announcements of course had some effect on the negotiations as delegates became more and more concerned about taking action.

Sometimes these scientific findings are communicated in side events during the COPs and intersessional negotiations.[224] These side events are not just distractions, but opportunities for delegates and other attendees to get the latest updates on the science. IPCC and WMO reports can be out of date by the time they are made available, but the side events bring scientists together to share the latest research.

Negotiations in Geneva

Negotiations opened on February 8 and continued to February 13, 2015. These negotiations were a continuation of the Lima negotiations, albeit at a lower diplomatic rank of negotiators. No heads of state and few foreign ministers attended. Co-Chairs Ahmed Djoghlaf (Algeria) and Daniel Reifsnyder (U.S.) of the "Working Group on Enhanced Action" identified the objective of the Geneva negotiations as narrowing down the negotiating text.[225]

While negotiations generally went well during the session, there were major issues left over from the Lima negotiations.

One of the key outputs from Lima was agreement on the requirements and process of intended nationally determined contributions (INDCs)... The Geneva text includes several proposals for the assessment of parties' commitments/contributions and the time frames and "cycles" for the submission of commitments. These apparently technical details are vital elements for ensuring what many have called a "dynamic agreement" that allows mitigation ambition to be periodically reviewed and strengthened after COP 21. Parties' views on this matter radically diverged.[226]

Because parties' views "radically diverged," negotiations during 2015 became quite contentious.

One of the major issues in these negotiations involves whether INDCs should be commitments without legal force. UK negotiators, along with others from Europe, favor legally binding commitments. Energy Secretary Ed Davey stated the UK position:

I want a comprehensive legally-binding treaty where it wouldn't just be the rules of the game, the accounting, monitoring, verification, all that, which are absolutely essential to be legally binding, I would like to see the commitments to be legally binding.[227]

Davey suggested that would be difficult for the U.S. to agree to binding commitments, which would mean that the U.S. have to get legislation through both houses of Congress, and for China, which could view it as a challenge to sovereignty.[228]

Davey put his finger on the main problems with the negotiations: the domestic political problems in the US and the issue of sovereignty for other nations such as China. These issues would come up frequently in the negotiations. The UK has had similar issues and its domestic politics could affect negotiations. Labor leader Ed Miliband has analyzed the climate issue through the lens of UK domestic politics.

Climate change has never been just an environmental issue. It affects the economy, migration and living standards too. There is no trade-off between tackling climate change and building an economy in which working families succeed. Indeed, success on one will help us achieve the other. Before the last election, the UK was a world leader in the transition to a green economy, with strong growth and investment in offshore wind turbine and nuclear power equipment manufacture. This government, which has long abandoned the pretence of being the "greenest ever", has cut and delayed investment in green technology. While Tory MPs flirt with climate change denial, confused and contradictory signals on energy policy from ministers have caused deep uncertainty for investors.[229]

Of course, Miliband is blaming the Tories for backtracking, but the UK like many other countries has its concerns with living standards that can militate against ambitious climate policies.

U.S. delegates suggested that the agreement leave out some of the specific commitments in the INDCs (see Chapter 3). While countries have described particular policies in their INDC submissions during the year, they will be revised as circumstances change. Those INDCs will also change over time and because the "ambitions" of parties, i.e., their increasing commitments to reducing emissions, will be changing, the INDC levels will probably increase as well.[230]

"Ambition" is the key term for encouraging member parties to adopt INDCs at levels sufficient to keep temperature increases below 2 degrees Celsius. In Geneva, some observers noted that, given what is known about negotiation positions, it is unlikely that current ambitions will meet that goal. "Announcements of planned post-2020 emission reductions by key emitters

China, the US and the EU have created concerns that the Paris Agreement will not be sufficiently ambitious to lead parties to a safe pathway towards the 2°C target."[231]

Alex Hanafi, an Environmental Defense Fund climate strategist who was in Geneva for the meetings, said, "More and more of the participants in the process recognize that maybe the 2 degree goal is not something that's going to be achieved out of the Paris Agreement. The idea is that the Paris Agreement will put us not on an emissions trajectory for 2 degrees, but on an institutional trajectory that allows us to try to meet that goal."[232] What is the "institutional trajectory" that can lead to that goal, a voluntary agreement or a legally binding one? That would be answered in subsequent negotiations leading to the Paris Agreement.

Some observers regard the voluntary option as the only realistic one. "It is apparent from these examples that an international climate treaty – voluntary or not – depends on the motivations of each participating country. Ultimately, domestic measures – laws, policies and regulations – are necessary to meet the international commitment. Many factors affect these national decisions, including each country's unique natural resources and economic and cultural circumstances, as well as the degree of its desire to be viewed as a responsible international actor."[233] Nevertheless, there are member parties that insisted on a legally binding agreement.

Nevertheless, EU delegates continued to raise the issue of a legally binding agreement.[234] According to a leaked document, EU negotiators want the Paris Agreement to be a "Paris Protocol," similar to the Kyoto Protocol. It would require member parties to commit to legally binding emissions cuts of 60% by 2050. It would go into effect as soon as countries with an 80% share of current emissions ratified it.[235]

The issue of a legally binding agreement has plagued negotiations since the original UNFCCC was signed and ratified in 1992. Because of the reluctance by the U.S. Congress to ratify the Kyoto Protocol, a legally binding agreement with some enforcement mechanisms, President Obama has stated his preference for an agreement that is based on voluntary enforcement. Many other parties are concerned that this will mean lax enforcement by some parties, often pointing fingers at the U.S., which has the second highest level of carbon emissions and by far the largest per-capita emissions.

"Ambitions" can differ according to the baseline against which they are measured. The different levels of emissions can be tabulated according to total CO_2 emissions by metric tons (tonnes) and tonnes per capita.[236]

Country	CO₂ Emissions	Emissions Per Capita
World	33,376,327	4.9
China	9,700,000	7.2
U.S.	5,420,000	17.3
India	1,970,000	1.6

Whether the U.S. will in fact lower its emissions to the world level or other countries will rise to the U.S. level was one of the most significant issues facing negotiators. Of course, the commitments described in Chapter 1 would lead to the decrease of U.S. emissions but by no means would they reach a level low enough to prevent temperature increases above 2 degrees Celsius. Some scientists say this would require all countries to lower per capita emissions to 2 tonnes per capita, just above the level of Indian emissions now. Unfortunately, it does not seem likely that even India will maintain that low level of emissions.

Another way to look at responsibility for emissions is the level of cumulative emissions. China has been responsible for about 10% of emissions since 1750, while the U.S. has been responsible for about 27%, three times as much. China and India together are responsible for about 13%, half as much as the U.S.[237]

Twin issues such as per capita emissions and cumulative emissions plague the negotiations. Developing countries point to the historical and current levels of emissions as an unfair advantage for developed countries, regardless of what they are doing or pledging to do now. Developed countries point to the overall emissions levels, and the accelerating pace of accumulation of carbon dioxide, as the common problem all member parties face. It is this common problem that challenges the world at the highest level and it must be addressed by all countries regardless of their historical role in climate change.

Issues of lowering emissions to a sustainable level feed prodigiously into denial ideology. Superficially, it would seem that we all have to reduce our standard of living to that of poor Indians, many of whom do not have access to electricity or clean water. This is obviously a massive simplification of the issues, when changes in energy production, transportation and manufacturing are all possible to sustain living standards alongside reduced emissions. Nevertheless, denial ideologues will argue that we all have to go back to hunting and gathering, curtail our consumption to caveman levels, and die off in enormous numbers to reduce emissions to a sustainable level.[238]

To some extent, this argument has validity, particularly in the writings of some energy analysts such as Richard Heinberg.

> Quite simply, we must learn to be successfully and happily poorer. For people in wealthy industrialized countries, this will require a major adjustment in thinking. When it comes to energy, we have deluded ourselves ... We must learn to operate within budgets and limits.[239]

While many would agree "we must learn to operate within budgets and limits," few acknowledge that this would mean "living poorer." Because of the delusion of thinking we can maintain our current patterns of consumption, continue to use fossil fuels at a growing rate, and avoid the consequences of climate change, denial ideology has a strong appeal.

Because of the sway of denial ideology in some societies, delegates in Geneva are hampered in efforts to reach an effective agreement. Other delegates have difficulties with issues carried over from previous negotiations. Some of the delegations were unhappy with the way that issues remaining from the Lima negotiations were incorporated into the new proposed text. Brazil objected to the phrase "evolving CBDR," referring to the phrase Common But Differentiated Responsibilities.[240] Developed member parties have often contended that CBDR is in fact evolving in the sense that developing countries such as Brazil are becoming more like developed countries in their economic development and need to take on responsibilities commensurate with their development.[241] The Brazilian delegate did not suggest that developing country parties would have no responsibilities, however.

While significant differences remained, the negotiations in Geneva did fulfill one of the expectations from the Lima COP: that the negotiation text was formally communicated to parties by March.[242] This enabled governments to review the text and develop positions for the next rounds of negotiations in Bonn, Germany in June, August and October.

Negotiations in Bonn – Round One

Negotiations in Bonn went from June 1 to June 11, 2015. UNFCCC Executive Director Christiana Figueres started off the negotiations with an optimistic view: "Instead of the blaming game that was Copenhagen, what is being built here is much more of an alliance, a broad collaboration among countries to get a deal together."[243] By comparing the current negotiations with Copenhagen, she may be trying to overcome the usual skepticism that greets leaders who are promoting an ambitious agreement.

Other observers were not so sanguine: "We went away happy from Geneva. But so did everyone else because no hard decisions were made. Bonn will be much tougher," according to a European diplomat.[244] French Foreign Minister Laurent Fabius referred to skepticism in the U.S. Congress in his observation about the need for careful negotiations: "we know the politics in the US. Whether we like it or not, if it comes to the Congress, they will refuse."[245]

The text left over from Geneva had 4,232 lines of text (90 pages) and hundreds of brackets, all of which will have to be agreed or deleted. Much of the Bonn session was devoted to debate over how to streamline the text.[246] The purpose of the Bonn negotiations was to narrow down the text with decisions on what home governments would accept for the final agreement in Paris. Early indications in the Bonn negotiations were not good: some delegations resisted the attempts by session co-Chairman Ahmed Djoghlaf (Algeria) to consolidate the text.[247]

Intended Nationally Determined Contributions (INDCs, see Chapter 3) were one key to successful negotiations. INDC pledges were made by 38 parties between the Lima COP in December 2014 and the Bonn negotiations in June 2015. By making the commitments voluntary and "intended," not legally binding, negotiators hoped to avoid some of the problems of the Kyoto Protocol, but this approach relied on the willingness of parties to make ambitious commitments and follow through on their commitments. Unfortunately, commitments made before Bonn have not been "ambitious" enough.

> None of the pledges, known in UN jargon as Intended Nationally Determined Contributions (INDCs), were found by Climate Analytics to be in line with the 2C limit, when a fair global distribution of emissions cuts was factored into countries' offers... "The action and ambition we have seen to date is far from sufficient and

unless it is rapidly accelerated, the difficulties of limiting warming below 2C will be extreme," said Dr. Bill Hare, the founder of Climate Analytics and a former Intergovernmental Panel on Climate Change (IPCC) lead author.[248]

According to pledges made by most large emitters, the earth would experience increased temperatures of 3.5C by 2100.[249] While this is better than the 4.5-degree increase projected on the basis of business as usual, it is still well above the 2C target. Nonetheless, by starting the process of making commitments, it is likely that member parties will strengthen their pledges as implementation of the agreement progresses. "By the time people get 10, 15 years of actually trying to do something, that's going to lead to greater expertise, better technology, more experience. People will then say, 'Oh, you know what? We can commit to do more,' " according to Gavin Schmidt, director of the NASA facility in Manhattan.[250]

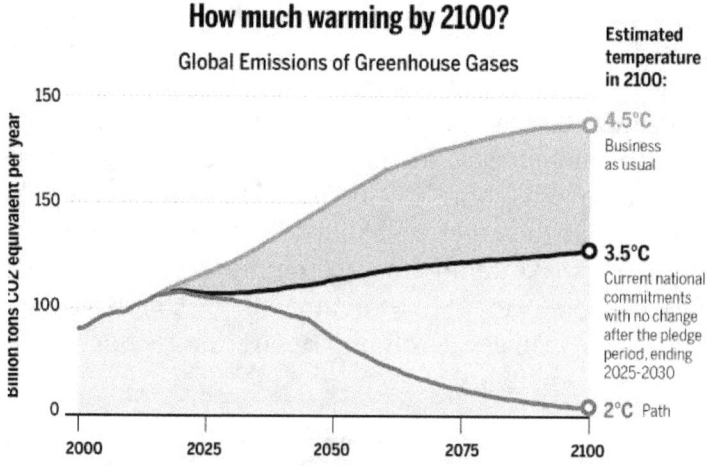

Source: climatescoreboard.org. Used by permission.

With most of the text bracketed, under negotiation, the diplomats in Bonn had to look beyond just the words to the overall objective of the agreement: to reduce carbon emissions to a level that would not be "dangerous anthropogenic interference with the climate system," to quote the text of the UNFCCC. Some observers did not think that the negotiations met this objective: "It's just not feasible," said Oliver Geden, of the German Institute for International and Security Affairs. "Two degrees is a focal point for the climate debate but it doesn't seem to be a focal point for political action."[251]

In the end, the first Bonn meeting had a rather minor success: the negotiation text was reduced from 90 to 85 pages. Co-chairs Dan Riefsnyder (U.S.) and Ahmed Djoghlaf (Algeria) were charged with further reducing the text by August, and some core issues were not resolved. Some observers thought these results were rather meager for two weeks of work – an EU delegate said "we must go faster."[252]

G7 Meeting

During the June 2015 meeting in Bonn, a two-day meeting of the G7 leaders took place 633 kilometers to the south in Krün, Germany, near Garmisch-Partenkirchen. G7 leaders include the presidents and prime ministers of Britain, Canada, France, Germany, Italy, Japan and the U.S., and the head of the EU Commission. Their communiqué at the end of the summit stated "We commit to doing our part to achieve a low-carbon global economy in the long-term, including developing and deploying innovative technologies striving for a transformation of the energy sectors by 2050, and invite all countries to join us in this endeavor." [253] The communiqué also committed G7 parties to reduce global greenhouse gas emissions to a range of 40% to 70% by 2050, using 2010 as a basis.

These commitments go beyond the INDCs announced before the Bonn negotiations, both in timing and level of ambition. For example, the INDCs do not specify beginning and end dates of 2010 and 2050. Further, the G7 commitments would extend their current levels, e.g. the U.S. committed to a 28% reduction by

2025, using 2005 as a basis. All of these goals depend for their implementation on continuation of policies by future leaders of some of the world's largest economies (excluding China and India, however). Such continuity is tenuous, given the vagaries of electoral politics.

Some of the discussion by G7 leaders in Krün differed from what governments had previously announced. A German delegate, for example, pointed to Germany's 40% emissions reduction target for 2020 compared to 1990 levels, and an 80-85% target for 2050.[254] Of course, Germany is free to indicate a more ambitious target than other G7 members, and has in the past exceeded EU commitments (partly due to closing down inefficient east German energy sources after the 1989 reunification). All of these discrepancies point to a core problem with the UNFCCC negotiations: the standards for setting targets and time commitments are so loose as to be practically nonexistent. To a great extent, this is deliberate so as to avoid the pitfalls of imposing legally binding commitments, as in the Kyoto Protocol, which fall by the wayside as parties fail to implement them.

A hint of this problem surfaced during discussions of even longer-term plans among G7 leaders. Canada and Japan objected to a statement that would commit the leaders to a zero-carbon economy by 2100. "Canada and Japan are the most concerned about this one. The two of those countries have been the most difficult on every issue on climate. They don't want any types of targets in there, so I think they are trying to make it as vague as possible at this point."[255]

If two of the G7 leaders can stymie the others with a long-term aspiration, not really a commitment, what are the prospects for the Paris Agreement? Obviously, the rather ephemeral goal of a zero-carbon future is not a hard commitment by present-day leaders, but they still express reservations. What will their multiple successors do?

Between Rounds One and Two in Bonn, on June 18, 2015, Pope Francis released an encyclical letter on climate change called *Laudato Si*. The encyclical was aimed at positioning the church and its members in favor of strong action at the Paris negotiations. The encyclical affirmed climate science: "A very solid scientific consensus indicates that we are presently witnessing a disturbing warming of the climatic system. ... A number of scientific studies indicate that most global warming in recent decades is due to the great concentration of greenhouse gases (carbon dioxide, methane, nitrogen oxides and others) released mainly as a result of human activity."[256] It called on diplomats to negotiate quickly an effective response: "enforceable international agreements are urgently needed."[257]

Some political leaders lauded the pope's encyclical. President Barack Obama said "As we prepare for global climate negotiations in Paris this December, it is my hope that all world leaders – and all of God's children – will reflect on Pope Francis' call to come together to care for our common home."[258] Political leaders could draw on the pope's message to support their own positions, but it also had the effect of stirring up denial ideology.

The encyclical on climate change brought the usual reactions from denial ideologues. Former Senator Rick Santorum, a candidate for president, said "The church has gotten it wrong a few times on science, and I think that we probably are better off leaving science to the scientists and focusing on what we're really good at, which is theology and morality. When we get involved with political and controversial scientific theories, I think the church is not as forceful and credible."[259] Santorum labels climate science *"controversial"* because he does not agree with it. Climate science is not controversial. The politics is controversial because he and other politicians find it necessary to oppose the policies to address climate change, such as the Obama administration's rules on coal-fired power plants.

Another Republican candidate for president, Marco Rubio, has taken the position that the pope can discuss moral issues but not political ones. He contends "humans are not responsible for climate change in the way some of these people out there are trying to make us believe."[260] By abnegating human responsibility he seems to think that there is no moral issue, only a political one – that advocates for climate policies are only trying to impose their policies without any scientific basis. This view depends on denial of well established human causes of climate change. His denial of the science, like that of many political leaders, relieves him of the difficult task of understanding and acting on the moral implications of climate change.

Some Republican strategists have gone even further than Santorum and Rubio in linking the pope's views to political ideology. Michael McKenna, a Republican energy lobbyist and political consultant, said:

> For practicing conservative Catholics, the folks who sit in the pews on Sunday, this is not going to be an indictment of guys like Rubio and Jeb [Bush]. Those guys have already made up their minds on climate change. For the real churchgoers, this is going to be an indictment of the pope. This pope is selling a line of Latin American-style socialism. This guy is not in sync with the American Catholic Church. Guys like Jeb and Rubio are more in line with the American Catholic Church than the pope.[261]

An *"indictment of the pope"* is a strong reaction to what is essentially an application of Catholic morality to climate change. [262] The encyclical letter is rather an indictment of politicians who try to avoid the moral implications of climate change by denying the science.

Jeb Bush, the third candidate from that family (his father and brother both became president), tried to sidetrack the pope's message by saying "But I don't get economic policy from my bishops or my cardinals or my pope. [Religion] ought to be about making us better as people, less about things [that] end up getting into the political realm." This is the same Bush that said in 2009, "As a public leader, one's faith should guide you."[263] So which is it, Mr. Bush: should religion stay out of the political realm or guide us in it?

Whatever the reaction, the pope's encyclical had the effect of stirring up the debate and put denial ideologues on notice that their views might not be popular. Its effect on policy was less certain, however, as the test of its effectiveness came in the negotiations in Bonn and Paris.

At the United Nations General Assembly in September 2015, the pope addressed the issue of poverty and related it to the misuse of the environment by wealthy countries. "The poorest are those who suffer most from such offenses, for three serious reasons: they are cast off by society, forced to live off what is discarded and suffer unjustly from the abuse of the environment."[264] While wealthy countries enjoy prosperity from use of fossil fuels, they "abuse the environment" through the carbon emissions that disproportionately affect the poor.[265]

Negotiations in Bonn – Round Two

Negotiations on the Paris text resumed in Bonn on August 31, 2015, and continued for a week. Technically, these negotiations are part of the "*Ad Hoc* Working Group on the Durban Platform for Enhanced Action," (ADP) a less formal setting than the Conference of Parties (COP21, Chapter 5). But their role is significant in setting the stage for COP21. On July 24, 2015, Co-Chairmen Reifsnyder and Djoghlaf had prepared an "informal note"[266] that set limits on the discussions. They tried to preempt delays in the proceedings by limiting the opening plenary to 30 minutes and requesting that delegations put their opening statements online. They recommended intensive use of the "contact group" mechanism to accelerate agreement on the text, so that delegates could speak freely (in closed sessions) without exposing themselves to outside criticism.

A major issue facing delegations during Round Two was how to handle the text, called a "tool," which the co-chairs divided into three parts: text crucial to the agreement, text that could be negotiated as part of a COP decision, and text that might be included in either of the above two rubrics. There was some grumbling that the co-chairs had narrowed the "crucial" text too severely,[267] but delegates seemed to welcome the clarifications. The co-chairs made clear that none of the text from Bonn Round One would be deleted, but by reorganizing it in this way, the negotiations could concentrate on what was most significant for the Paris Agreement.

Another issue, left over from the Warsaw COP19 (2013), was how to handle "loss and damage." The concept that member parties could suffer loss and damage from climate change induced by other member parties would open the international system to a slew of litigation, as parties tried to establish who was responsible and now much they should pay. While the G77 tried to negotiate institutional arrangements for managing loss and damage, others such as the U.S. proposed leaving it to COP decisions that carry less weight.[268] This compromise would mean that loss and damage could be left out of the Paris Agreement.

The issue of "loss and damage" folds into the issue of finance. The pledge by developed country parties to fund the Green Climate Fund at a level of $100 billion a year is still pending because the deadline for it to reach that level is 2020. Presumably this funding could cover loss and damage as it is intended to pay for adaptation as well as mitigation. But that issue was not settled in Bonn. Agricultural losses from droughts and infrastructure losses from floods, for example, could be compensated by adaptation of crops to drought conditions, or rebuilding the infrastructure to withstand floods, both of which could be considered adaptation. Success of the Paris Agreement hinged on resolving the issue of finance. Host President Francois Hollande has said, "There will not be an agreement if there is no firm commitment on financing."[269]

As a result of an impasse on "loss and damage," some observers regarded negotiations in Bonn, Round Two, as less than successful. "The US and EU took baby steps towards agreeing to deal with climate damages for vulnerable countries, but insisted on leaving this out of the core agreement. Its exclusion will likely cripple a deal in Paris," according to Harjeet Singh, climate policy manager at ActionAid.[270] The U.S. has called for leaving the issue open for later discussion. "From the perspective of the rich countries, it looks like unlimited liability for bad weather. That could get in the way of agreement," according to Robert Stavins, a Harvard University economics professor.[271] Whether it is incorporated into the Paris Agreement is a factor in the success of the pact.

This issue, and many others, raised the specter of what some delegates call "binary issues."[272] In essence, this refers to the divide between developed and developing countries on such questions as mitigation ambitions (INDCs) and differentiated responsibilities (CBDR, see Chapter 3). It particularly impacts discussion of finance because of the view that developed countries bear a greater responsibility for past emissions, which can be discharged through financial support for developing countries.

Other negotiators lamented the slow pace of the negotiations. "We are aware that progress has been insufficient and uneven. Three months before Paris, the pace is slow and the current tool is evidently not the best suitable for effective deliberations," according to Jorge Voto Bernales, special representative of Peru for climate change.[273] It is not unusual for delegates to complain about the pace of negotiations; often the text is not fully agreed until the last minute. But the leadership of UNFCCC does not consider this a major problem. "Of course we're all impatient. Of course we're all frustrated. While the frustration and impatience is absolutely a reality, this does take the time that it takes... It is ultimately the outcome that is the important thing," according to Executive Secretary Christiana Figueres.[274] Her sentiments were echoed by Ahmed Djoghlaf, co-chair for the Bonn meeting, who said "We are making progress. ... We will be on time in Paris."[275]

A broader question is how the negotiations in Bonn reflect the larger issues facing member parties. An analysis of the outcome of Bonn, Round Two, indicates that there is a "disconnect between the technical negotiations within the UNFCCC from the political processes happening outside the UNFCCC."[276] Although these "political processes" are not spelled out, it is likely that they include domestic pressures on the negotiators as well as the international politics represented in events such as a summit meeting of the G7 in Krün, Germany and release of the Pope's encyclical *Laudato Si,* both in June (discussed above). Nevertheless, the building momentum for agreement was not so manifest in the slow pace of negotiations in Bonn, Round Two. It remains to be seen if talks will accelerate in Bonn in October for the next round, the last before Paris.

Negotiations in Bonn – Round Three

Negotiations on the Paris text resumed in Bonn on October 19, 2015, and continued for a week. Technically, these negotiations are also part of the *"Ad Hoc* Working Group on the Durban Platform for Enhanced Action," as noted above. Delegates were asked to concentrate on narrowing the text that would be taken up by high-level officials in Paris. This proved to be a thankless task.

Co-chairman Dan Reifsnyder opened the negotiations with a new text[277] that did not have complete consensus, but he suggested that delegates could make "surgical insertions" of their must-have text.[278] The text had been slimmed down from 85 pages (Geneva text) to 21 pages. Reifsnyder encountered some resistance to this approach, but delegates proceeded to discuss the text. "Even though parties agreed to make only essential 'surgical insertions' into the Co-Chairs' text, many used the compilation process as a means to re-introduce their long-held positions into the text."[279] This meant that the text ballooned from 21 to 55 pages when parties added provisions that had to be bracketed. "So while many welcomed the restoration of parties' ownership of the text, even more worried that delegates in Paris had been saddled with an impossible task."[280]

Small-island states were particularly concerned that the text did not go far enough to prevent inundation of their countries.[281] Some member parties preferred 1.5 degrees to the 2-degree limit adopted in Cancun[282] (See Chapter 1). Nevertheless, many parties including Switzerland and the EU supported the co-chairman's approach. Some, such as Australia, suggested that too many "surgical insertions" would make the text too unwieldy for negotiation in Paris. [283] Throughout the week, there were many efforts to add text while delegates struggled with streamlining the agreement to make it more useful for high-level negotiations in Paris.

Developing countries at first were incensed that the text did not contain more details on finance, a recurring issue throughout Bonn negotiations. "Developed countries have not negotiated, in the hope that [finance] will be sorted externally of the agreement where we are weakest, and it translates into ODA as opposed to the obligations that must be put here - and the reason why they don't want civil society in, because that's where they hope they will get away with it," according to Ambassador Nozipho Mxakato-Diseko of South Africa.[284]

Finance continued to be an issue as developing countries opposed the notion that developed countries have already contributed $62 billion in climate aid. Some, including India, questioned the accounting by the OECD (Organization for Economic Cooperation and Development). "Suggesting creative accounting and green-washing of existing global fund flows to paint a more rosy rather a real picture." [285] Nevertheless, developed countries continued to insist that all financial flows to developed countries be counted, including private investment, if they contribute to "green energy."

One issue that has persisted throughout the negotiation rounds in Bonn is "loss and damage." (See Chapter 3) Parties disagreed as to whether it should be included in the agreement or a COP decision.[286] Including it in the agreement would give parties more credibility in bringing actions against polluters, but such actions would raise issues of international law. [287] Some developing country delegates accused developed country delegates of denial: "It is deeply concerning for us when we hear the calls not to include this issue in the discussions [of the agreement text]," said Juan Hoffmaister from Bolivia. "Because at this stage with the science and the knowledge we have available, to talk about not having loss and damage is the equivalent to climate denial."[288] This issue was postponed until Paris when higher-level delegates commit their governments to a position. (See Chapter 5)

Because the text was still heavily bracketed and had "surgical insertions" on which not all parties agreed, it was not quite what the co-chairmen envisioned for Paris. Delegates in Bonn had to find common ground among themselves and then sell the text to their home governments, but as one delegate put it near the end of the session, "what we have currently is not a text I can deliver to my minister." [289] Without ownership by all parties, the text brought to Paris was to cause considerable difficulties for high-level negotiations.

Bonn negotiations and the heavily bracketed text stimulated some heavy criticism. Craig Rucker, executive director and co-founder of CFACT, made several denial arguments.[290]

- ...130 developing nations – "led by South Africa and instigated by China and India" – are insisting they will not sign a climate deal in Paris unless it contains massive redistribution of wealth from developed to poor nations.

- "Whatever they call it, countries who sign onto this agreement will be voting to expand the reach of the U.N. climate bureaucracy, cede national sovereignty, and create a one-way street along which billions will be redistributed from developed to poor nations."

- "Now they want the power to haul the U.S. and its allies before a U.N. Star Chamber to enforce compliance."

Of course, some of the bracketed text to which CFACT refers is not in the final agreement. As to the *"redistribution of income"* issue, the finance sections of the agreement do provide for climate aid to developing countries. One could argue that this aid is to the benefit of all countries, as the restructuring of the energy system in any one country can enhance the climate stability of all countries.

With regard to the *"U.N. Star Chamber,"* the Paris Agreement has no enforcement mechanisms that could be called "star chambers." (See Chapter 6 for further discussion of enforcement) As a voluntary agreement, the Paris Agreement lacks "teeth" and depends entirely on the policies of member parties to implement the INDCs. Five-year reviews can be considered a form of enforcement but they rely only on publicity and "shaming" and have no sanctions.

Climate Change and Terrorism

Shortly before the Paris COP21 began on November 30, a group affiliated with ISIS (Islamic State in Iraq and Syria, also known as ISIL, Islamic State in the Levant) attacked cafes and a sports stadium in Paris, killing 130 people and injuring hundreds more. Some observers saw this as an attempt to sabotage the conference, although the French government vowed to carry on with the COP and beefed up security. Unfortunately, the incident did result in much more strict limits on demonstrations and activities of civil society, causing a number of non-governmental organizations to cancel their attendance or drastically alter their plans.

What does ISIS have to do with climate change? "It's a pretty convincing climate fingerprint – you can draw a very credible climate connection to this disaster we call ISIS right now," according to Retired Navy Rear Admiral David Titley, a meteorologist by training.[291] The Department of Defense has issued warnings in its annual reports that climate change is a "threat multiplier" by causing unrest and contributing to conflicts.

In the U.S., the possible link of climate change and terrorism became a major political issue and aroused strong reactions. ISIS claimed responsibility for the Paris attacks in November 2015, and indeed some of the attackers had been trained in Syria. Some governors vowed to keep all Syrian refuges out of their states, while others said they would welcome them. Senator Bernie Sanders (I-VT), running for president, answered a question at the November Democratic debate about his highest priority for world affairs. He maintained his stance that climate change is the highest priority, and went on to say that terrorism and refugee migrations often stem from climate change, as for example, the drought in Syria for several years before the uprising there that led to mass migration and the establishment of ISIS.

Predictably, the issue of climate change and terrorism aroused much of the heated rhetoric that infuses denial ideology. Marc Morano, former aide to Senator James Inhofe and head of the "climate depot" blog, said, "They are desperately trying to link 'global warming' to terrorism or come up with conspiracy theories on how Big Oil interests may be behind the terror attacks. The climate activists are now trying to rebrand the U.N. climate summit as some sort of 'peace summit' where addressing 'global warming' will somehow solve terrorism and civil wars."[292] Of course, claiming that it will solve terrorism or civil wars has never been inherent in climate science. Climate action may address some of the root causes of civil unrest if the effects of drought and extreme weather are alleviated, but the issue of terrorism has always been a political-military issue, not a science issue.

After the Paris attack, Cornwall Alliance caricatured world leaders and negotiators: "I will remind you that President Obama has stated that the threat of climate change is greater than the threat of terrorism. I will also remind you that many believe that ISIS would not have arisen if not for climate change, specifically, drought in Syria caused by your SUV."[293] This caricature seems to imply that leaders assert that if Americans do not stop driving SUVs, terror attacks might continue.

Cornwall Alliance goes on to say, "It is only logical that ISIS should be supportive of COP21 in Paris, and that the conference should go on as planned. To enlightened minds, terrorism is clearly just a consequence of climate change. Fix the weather, and terrorism will go away. If terrorism is such a minor, contained threat (as Obama just stated yesterday), and global warming is really the overriding threat facing humanity, how can we consider cancelling – or even postponing – COP21? After all, isn't COP21 our last, final, last chance to Save the Earth?"[294] Here the caricature descends to the level of suggesting COP21 is supported by ISIS and is some kind of last hurrah for climate science, and that its success or failure will determine for all time the fate of the earth. This rather cartoonish portrayal shows the facetious nature of Cornwall Alliance analyses.

Cornwall Alliance then reaches an absurd level of caricature about international negotiations. "Just ignore centuries of history which demonstrates that the strict followers of the Koran have a holy mandate to take over the world for Islam, killing anyone who will not submit. Yes, all of the world's politicians who have supported a COP21 agreement should still plan on attending. And they should reach out to ISIS to join them in building a better world...a world without droughts. In fact, in solidarity with the gun-control measures many of those politicians support (and which French law follows), any personal security personnel accompanying them should be unarmed."[295] The rhetoric drags in the old saw about how gun control makes negotiators more vulnerable because they (and the security forces that guard them) will not be armed. It is a tongue-in-cheek suggestion that climate negotiators are somehow clueless diplomats and world leaders who would reach out to ISIS to join them.

Chapter 5
Negotiations in Paris

"We all need to have Paris succeed – all of us in the negotiations, just people around the world generally. I think people will conclude that if you can't deliver an agreement in Paris that you're going to start looking around for other ways to find international solutions." Todd Stern, U.S. envoy for climate change negotiations.[296]

Now it's time for other nations to come forward with their own targets, and to make it possible to reach a meaningful global agreement at the UN Climate Conference in Paris later this year. We need every country on the same page, all pushing for an ambitious, durable, and inclusive agreement that will finally put us on the path towards a global clean-energy future. Failure is not an option. Secretary of State John Kerry.[297]

There is "no plan B – nothing to follow. This is not just ongoing UN discussions. Paris is final." Miguel Cañete, Commissioner for Climate Action, European Union[298]

In the following sections, text without footnotes is from personal observation. There are references to the text of the Paris Agreement; the full text can be found in the Appendix.

The Setting

Le Bourget, the airport where Charles Lindbergh landed at the end of his historic flight in 1927, was the first airport in France. Today it hosts a number of private corporate jets but no commercial flights. The hangars not used by corporate jets have been reconstructed as meeting halls, and they can hold a large number of people in multiple meetings. That was a good setting for COP21 which had over 36,000 participants.

The French had organized COP 21 well. They set up two enormous tents, each the size of a football field, to handle the large crowds of attendees. One was a security tent with more than 20 security lines to facilitate entry, a problem that had plagued earlier COPs such as Copenhagen. Of course, the French were also being extra cautious with security after the Paris massacre (See Chapter 4) with police and soldiers evident everywhere around the conference site. A second tent held all of the "civil society" groups that tend to flock around COPs. This tended to drain off some of the actions that might be disruptive to the main conference buildings. The French had also, in cooperation with the UNFCCC secretariat, planned the conference schedule in a way to insure success. Having heads of state and heads of government appear at the beginning, rather than the end, helped get some of the rhetoric and posturing out of the way early. The conference was also designed some years in advance to be the end stage of the "Ad Hoc Working Group on the Durban Platform of Enhanced Action" (mercifully shortened to the acronym ADP). ADP did in fact end its work on December 5, in time to compile a text for the negotiations beginning on December 7 with the oversight of government ministers, both foreign ministers and environmental ministers. ADP, whose work has been described in more detail in Chapter 4, was the "working level" group that actually came up with the text after five grueling sessions. Its final session was in fact the first week of COP21, when work sessions were held in parallel with the high-level speeches. The text was whittled down from 54 pages to a final agreed text of 31 pages and some of the disputes over wording were settled with "bridging proposals," that is, links between similar wording by different parties.

The French adopted some interesting tactics for the second week of negotiations. Laurence Tubiana, the French Ambassador for Climate Change, set up a "Paris

Committee" with five subcommittees to handle the main issues such as mitigation pledges and finance. Each is chaired by two foreign ministers, one from developed countries and the other from developing countries. They thrashed out the text for each areas and brought it back to the plenaries for final decisions.

Negotiations

Negotiations in Paris began early, on Sunday November 29, 2015, a day ahead of the opening of COP21. The Sunday negotiations were the final meeting of the ADP, the group that had met throughout 2015 in Geneva and Bonn. (Chapter 4) At the ADP session, delegates reviewed the text that came out of the previous four ADP sessions. No decisions were made, but the review was an essential step in preparing for the decisions that would be made by the higher-level delegations.[299]

ADP Co-Chair Dan Reifsnyder referred to text, called "informal note," that had been issued in November (ADP.2015.10-12.InformalNote). He said that a consolidated new draft would be prepared by Friday, December 4, and the outcome of the ADP would be forwarded to the COP for its consideration on Saturday, December 5.[300] These stratagems illustrated the *modus operandi* of COP21, which was to focus on streamlining text already discussed in the intersessional meetings and removing brackets as delegations agreed on common text.

In their discussion of the text, the delegates tended to link issues such as INDCs, CBDRs and Finance. Negotiations are reviewed below based on these linkages. Where appropriate, statements by heads of state in the first week are reviewed in the context of the negotiations on these issues. During the final week, negotiations got down to wordsmithing the text that was agreed on December 12, 2015.

INDCs and CBDR

Negotiations began with discussions of INDCs (Intended Nationally Determined Contributions, see Chapter 3). At the outset developing nations invoked the principle of CBDR (common but differentiated responsibilities, see Chapters 3 and 4). India indicated that developing countries were likely to have different INDCs than developed countries: "Justice demands that, with what little carbon we can still safely burn, developing countries are allowed to grow. The life styles of a few [developed countries] must not crowd out opportunities for the many still on the first steps of the development ladder."[301]

President Xi Jinping of China echoed this sentiment: "Addressing climate change should not deny the legitimate needs of developing nations to reduce poverty and improve their people's living standards."[302] President Dilma Rouseff of Brazil emphasized (CBDR) as the cornerstone of the Paris Agreement.[303] As one of the emerging economies, Brazil will have an important role in the transition from a dualistic CBDR toward the more flexible concept of "concentric circles." (See Chapter 3) Chancellor Angela Merkel of Germany proposed a binding review mechanism with a five-year cycle to begin in 2020 to ensure credibility and increased ambition of the INDC pledges.[304] This would stiffen the concept of five-year reviews by making it binding, a suggestion that may arouse opposition from some member parties. President Vladimir Putin of the Russian Federation also proposed that the agreement be legally binding, a nonstarter for the U.S. (see Chapter 3)

As expected, some parties such as the small-island states called for keeping global temperature rise below 1.5 degrees Celsius, instead of the 2C limit agreed in Cancun. The Maldives, which has taken the lead in pushing for the lower limit, called for the agreement to set medium- and long-term emission reduction pathways at levels less than 1.5C of warming.[305]

One issue that arose during the negotiations was the gap between INDCs proposed by approximately 180 member parties, and the level of emission reductions required to attain the 2C target. ADP Co-Chair Daniel Reifsnyder suggested mentioning the gap resulting from the aggregate effect of INDCs communicated by parties as of October 2015. (See Chapter 4) He proposed inserting figures to illustrate the gap and including language from the Intergovernmental Panel on Climate Change on lowest-cost emission pathways.[306] If adopted, this proposal could create dissent as member parties might be reluctant to show how they have fallen short. Member parties seemed to favor "taking note" of the gaps rather than incorporating any text into the agreement.[307]

Some parties continued to press for 1.5°C limits. Tuvalu, one of the small island states affected by sea-level rise, suggested that the IPCC (Intergovernmental Panel on Climate Change) analyze the INDCs and compare them to the level of emissions reductions required for the 1.5°C limit. Saudi Arabia and other member parties questioned the value of such analysis, beyond the already-available information from IPCC reports.[308]

One party, Nicaragua, indicated some hostility to the way that the agreement handled the question of INDC commitments. Nicaragua called for a "carbon budget" (see Chapter 6), which would allocate emissions based on a worldwide limit and criteria of "fairness" in allotting carbon distribution by country. This concept did not have much traction from most of the parties, however.

In the end, the agreement included the 1.5°C limit as an aspiration: "Holding the increase in the global average temperature to well below 2°C above pre-industrial levels and to pursue efforts to limit the temperature increase to 1.5°C above pre-industrial levels..." (See Appendix for full wording of the agreement). Some countries, such as Maldives speaking for small island states, emphasized that 1.5 °C is essential for the survival of low-lying states.

Finance and CBDR

Finance became an early issue in the negotiations, just as it had been throughout the intersessional meetings. "The cost of action is not $100 billion," said Prakash

Javadekar, the Indian environment minister. "It is trillions; $100 billion is just a reparation."[309] Talk of "reparations" is likely to set the teeth of some delegates on edge, as this arouses all of the problems of CBDR discussed earlier (Chapters 1, 3 and 4). President Obama in his speech to delegates did acknowledge the burden on developed countries: "We know the truth that many nations have contributed little to climate change but will be the first to feel its most destructive effects."[310]

A recurring issue on financial responsibility surfaced in Paris. The EU and the US agreed that developed countries should meet their financial obligations, and that others in a position to do so should contribute. [311] This was a reference to emerging economies such as China that are in a position to contribute to the Green Climate Fund, which is intended to help less developed countries mitigate emissions and adapt to climate change. The EU emphasized that its commitment to mobilize climate finance would continue after 2020 and the $100 billion commitment could be scaled up with an expansion of the donor base. [312] Contributions by all countries in a position to help are a key to the success of the agreement.

In the end, the agreement did mention finance in the text of the agreement but kept the $100 billion figure in the accompanied COP decision (See Appendix). Compare text from the COP decision to the text in the agreement:

> *COP Decision*: in accordance with Article 9, paragraph 3, of the Agreement, developed countries intend to continue their existing collective mobilization goal through 2025 in the context of meaningful mitigation actions and transparency on implementation; prior to 2025 the Conference of the Parties serving as the meeting of the Parties to the Paris Agreement shall set a new collective quantified goal from a floor of USD 100

billion per year, taking into account the needs and priorities of developing countries.

Agreement: Developed country Parties shall provide financial resources to assist developing country Parties with respect to both mitigation and adaptation in continuation of their existing obligations under the Convention.

Finance provisions of the agreement are administered through the Green Climate Fund. The GCF has already been in operation and has a number of features:

- The initial mobilization is $10.2 billion;

- Commitments are allocated for a 50-50 balance between mitigation and adaptation;

- More than 50% of adaptation funding goes to most vulnerable countries including small island states;

- Direct private sector engagement is through the Private Sector Facility;

- Risk-bearing capacity allows for innovation and leverage in additional funding;

- A variety of financial instruments are available including concessional loans, debt equity, and grants.

In the end, the Paris Agreement leaves open the question of how parties will divide up the $100 billion obligation, and how developing countries will use the funds. Developed country parties are concerned about the accountability of the funds and want as much as possible to be used for mitigation, not adaptation. Developing country parties are facing immediate crises of adaptation, and want the flexibility of using the funds for crises as they arise.

Closing Plenary

President Francois Hollande and UN Secretary General Ban Ki-Moon accompanied Foreign Minister Laurent Fabius, the COP21 president, for the final plenary on December 12. Fabius declared the text agreed and all the delegates celebrated with cheers and hugs.

Fabius commended facilitators of sessions on transparency, ambition and compromise; they had managed to overcome differences in order to complete the text. He said it is a balanced text with principles of differentiated, fair, dynamic and legally binding provisions; and the text acknowledges climate justice. It affirms the objective of keeping increasing temperatures below 2C and strives to limit them to 1.5C. The agreement has made it the business of all parties to keeping their commitments by subjecting them to review every 5 years; and increased role of cooperation of parties on funding adaptation and loss and damage.

Fabius acknowledged that the negotiations were difficult. Each party put forth proposals and set red lines; but not everyone was able to attain all they wanted. He said that negotiations succeeded because parties tended to focus on green lines, not red lines and all can go home with head held high. He quoted Nelson Mandela: "it always seems impossible until it is done."

UN Secretary-General Ban Ki-Moon spoke next. He thanked Fabius and Hollande for guiding negotiations. He said that the agreement will set the world on the path to low-carbon future. He thanked delegations who brought us so far and were able to finish the job, while the whole world was watching. He said that their various national interests are served by acting in common interest. He said he had talked with all leaders about completing this agreement and they have responded with positive support. He called on parties to provide financial support for developing countries and embark on low emissions pathway, and asked developing countries to continue on low carbon development.

Finally, French President Francois Hollande spoke. He said that the international community has proved that it can act. He noted that hard work has been done, day and night, and we now have a universal agreement that is differentiated and legally binding. He commended delegations for overcoming gridlock on international cooperation. The agreement text is ambitious and realistic, and reconciles responsibility of richest countries while includes differentiation for developing countries. He said the Paris Agreement is the first universal climate agreement of history. The Paris Agreement cannot satisfy all imperatives and claims, but we will not be judged on the text but on the whole approach and its implications for the future. An agreement among 196 delegations is unprecedented. He said that we can be sure there will be opposition, but with this agreement you have the opportunity to change the world.

Many delegations spoke in similar vein. Among the delegation heads, Secretary of State John Kerry said that delegations had provided critical multilateral stewardship and the agreement is a victory for all citizens of world, victory for the planet and for future generations. He noted that of 196 delegations, 186 parties had submitted emission reduction plans, which represents remarkable global commitment. There are things everybody doesn't like, but the agreement will prepare us for changes coming, including a transition to a clean energy economy and a way to prevent the worst effects of climate change. He said that we are sending a signal to the markets, where the genius of the American spirit of innovation will provide solutions. He expressed gratitude to France, on behalf of President Obama, for setting an example to world. He said that some may not like it but the Paris Agreement is in the interests of the earth. We will leave legacy for children and grandchildren better than we would otherwise.

Virtually all delegations lauded the success of the Paris Agreement, except for the delegation from Nicaragua, as noted earlier.

Did Paris Succeed?

But did Paris succeed? Some climate activists do not think so. James Hansen, former director of the Goddard Institute for Space Studies and a notable leader of climate campaigns such as the Keystone XL Pipeline demonstrations, said "This [agreement] is half-assed and it's half-baked" because it would allow emissions to increase, albeit at a slower rate.[313] He prefers a carbon tax rather than pledges to reduce emissions. Hansen's position is laudable but perhaps a little unrealistic.

Some climate activists were even more derisive than Hansen. Friends of the Earth International, in a statement released on December 12, 2015, said "The climate deal to be agreed today is a sham. Rich countries have moved the goal posts so far that we are left with a sham of a denial." Naomi Klein said, "The deal unveiled [December 12], to much fanfare and self-congratulation from politicians, echoed by an overly deferential press, will not be enough to keep us safe. In fact, it will be extraordinarily dangerous. We know, from doing the math and adding up the targets that the major economies have brought to Paris, that those targets lead us to a very dangerous future. They lead us to a future between 3 and 4 degrees Celsius warming."[314] While some opposed the agreement as too weak, others considered it too tough.

The campaign of Governor John Kasich of Ohio released a statement: "While the governor believes that climate change is real and that human activity contributes to it, he has serious concerns with an agreement that the Obama administration deliberately crafted to avoid having to submit it to the Senate for approval. That's an obvious indicator that they expect it to result in significant job loss and inflict further damage to our already sluggish economy."[315] This is a typical, albeit mild, form of the familiar canard that climate action means job losses. It attributes nefarious motives to the Obama administration for crafting the agreement to avoid Senate review. It does not directly address the substance of the agreement itself.

Another presidential candidate, Senator Marco Rubio (R-FL), said the agreement was an "unfunny joke of a climate deal" and "[China is] going to keep that deal so long as it doesn't hurt their ability to grow their economy," an echo of earlier statements by U.S. politicians who apparently have not heard that China is already starting to lower emissions. Senator Ted Cruz (R-TX) said he would withdraw the U.S. from the agreement if elected president.

Senate Majority Leader Mitch McConnell (R-KY) described the accord as "nothing more than a long-term planning document. The president is making promises he can't keep, writing checks he can't cash and stepping over the middle class to take credit for an agreement that is subject to being shredded in 13 months." [316] McConnell is of course referring to the possibility that a Republican president would be elected in 2016 and renege on the agreement.

"Lukewarmers" predicted that the Paris Agreement would fail.

> Despite what [was] committed to paper or alluded to during the self-congratulatory ceremony at the conclusion of the Paris conference (just as has happened many times before), this one like all the others is likely to fail. Here's why. Greenhouse gas emissions result from the combustion of fossil fuels. Those combustion processes are the primary source of energy powering the modern economy. Once a nation's population comes to enjoy a modern economy, they want to keep it rolling. Those without one want one, pronto. Consequently, global CO_2 emissions will

continue to rise despite any flowery talk that emanates from Paris during COP-21.[317]

Contending that the developing countries will want to attain as high a standard of living as developed countries, and both will need to burn fossil fuel to maintain it, is an argument repeated many times in the denial literature. It rests on the premise that there is no way of avoiding the increased use of fossil fuels, a narrow view at best and a pernicious disavowal of technical and social change at worst.

Cornwall Alliance repeated its canard about how action on climate change harms the poor: "But to the extent that the Paris Agreement actually gets implemented, it's a disaster for the poor around the world. It will slow their access to the abundant, affordable, reliable energy indispensable to rising and staying out of poverty, while achieving no discernable improvement in climate but diverting trillions of dollars from solving hunger, malnutrition, and disease."[318] This sentiment was echoed in an open letter written by a group of denialists, as reported by Fox News: "Proposals to fight climate change doom billions of people to live in extreme poverty, a fate much worse than global warming."[319]

Despite the best efforts of the denial industry, however, people generally support climate agreements. "...in 37 out of the 40 countries Pew surveyed, the number of people who support limiting carbon dioxide emissions as part of an international agreement exceeds the number who think climate change is a serious problem." [320] Climate change can be a low-priority problem for people who are more concerned about immediate issues such as poverty and terrorism. But most people around the world recognize that climate change is an issue that must be addressed, and they are willing to support international efforts such as the Paris Agreement. Nevertheless, there are those who persist in opposing the agreement. Politicians take advantage of this feeling that climate change is a low priority: "While the world is in turmoil and falling apart in so many different ways especially with ISIS, our President is worried global warming – what a ridiculous situation," said U.S. presidential candidate Donald Trump.[321]

Sometimes the criticism of the agreement comes in milder doses. Patrick Michaels and Paul Knappenberger contend that "Despite the hurricane of self-congratulatory hoopla ... [that did] accompany the end of the Paris fetê, close analysis will reveal a climate agreement that will accomplish little even as it may cost a lot. It will be a lukewarm agreement, as is fitting for a lukewarm world."[322] Of course, they have a point: the Paris Agreement does not fully address the issue of how to keep global temperature rise below 2C, but that is not important for them. They think that a little warming is a good thing, and the Paris Agreement is unnecessary.

Some negotiators were more optimistic. Todd Stern, the chief U.S. negotiator, suggested that the Paris negotiations were better than the failed Copenhagen negotiations in 2009. "We are in a different place than we were in Copenhagen. I think there is a greater level of convergence on some very important structural issues with respect to the agreement than existed in Copenhagen." [323] It was unclear what he meant by "structural issues," but the U.S. maintained the stance of voluntary commitments for the Paris negotiations while in Copenhagen some negotiators were seeking legally binding commitments.

The EU has taken strong positions on climate change during past negotiations and did so in these negotiations. Mayors of EU cities, for example, issued the following statement:

Since the Earth Summit in Rio de Janeiro in 1992, 23 years ago, the United Nations has been trying to achieve an international consensus on the issue of climate change while its effects continue to worsen. Today, we have no alternative. The ... climate summit in Paris in December 2015 must show that we are

107

fully aware of what is at stake. European metropolises are already acting by proposing local solutions to tackle climate change.[324]

The EU's position clashed with other parties as the question of legally binding commitments is debated (see Chapter 3), but EU member parties do have the moral high ground because of their recent successes in reducing emissions.[325]

Regardless of the arguments for legally binding commitments to emissions reductions, the Paris Agreement does not incorporate any such language. The reasoning for the voluntary nature of the agreement is clear: it is much more feasible than any binding legal instrument. Stern notes that: "There is an emerging consensus that to overcome the emissions gap, any ... agreement will need to be dynamic in the sense of including processes for revising commitments upward over time, and collaborative in the sense of fostering a shared commitment among countries to work together to achieve a mutually beneficial transition to a low-carbon world, with strong, high-quality growth and poverty reduction at its heart." He contrasts this dynamic approach to the more legalistic, static approach adopted for the Kyoto Protocol: "This is a very different approach from trying to agree on a centralized and legalistic framework that 'solves' climate change by attempting to bind countries to ambitious emissions reductions once and for all." [326] While there is a risk to relying on voluntary compliance with nationally determined goals, the very fact that the goals are announced and reviewed by other parties does provide some gravitas to the commitments.

Findings of climate science drive negotiations and the principal vehicle for conveying these findings to the negotiators is the IPCC (Intergovernmental Panel on Climate Change). IPCC produced a major assessment report in 2013 and 2014, the conclusions of which indicated that manmade climate change is definite and accelerating.[327] These assessment reports, and the science on which they are based, are often attacked by denial ideologues. [328] Sometimes these attacks extend to denouncing the negotiations themselves.

> The 2013-14 IPCC assessment report does its best to ramp up the alarmism in a desperate, and almost certainly vain, attempt to scare the governments of the world into concluding a binding global decarbonisation agreement at the crunch UN climate conference … in Paris, 2015. Yet a careful reading of the report shows that the evidence to justify the alarm simply isn't there.[329]

It is doubtful that the IPCC reports "scared" governments into concluding an unjustified agreement, but the reports did impel governments to agree that emissions must be reduced.[330] How they implement that decision was a major question following the negotiations. If they succumb to the influence of the denial industry, the implementation measures may be less effective than otherwise.

One reason that governments may be impelled to address climate change is that conflicts over energy use have increased in recent years. After outlining a number of the conflicts, French Foreign Minister Laurent Fabius said, "it is essential for COP21 to provide – first and foremost to developing countries – the practical means to increase access to energy, while reducing the carbon intensity of economies. This would decrease considerably the risk of fossil fuels becoming a cause of conflict in the coming decades."[331] He was referring to complementary provisions of the agreement, reduction of carbon emissions in developing countries and provision of funds to implement these reductions by developed countries.

The form of the Paris Agreement was complex. "The Paris package [was] a mix of legal and political outcomes, contained in a variety of instruments, addressing both pre-2020 ambition and the post-2020 framework. These include: a core agreement; parties' intended nationally determined contributions (INDCs), whether in, referenced in and/or accompanying the core agreement; related decisions of the Conference of the Parties (COP); and one or more political declarations."[332] While it is difficult to separate the elements of an agreement in the public arena, the diplomats are well aware of the different effects of each.

Although the Paris negotiations were a limited success, many felt that the process of setting targets (INDCs) and addressing the means of achieving them were important steps. Because the changes in climate are coming at a rapid pace, more rapid than some scientists anticipated, the review and renewal of commitments was an important part of the process. One expert who proposed five-year cycles of review, Fatih Birol, executive director of the International Energy Agency, said: "The pledges in Paris need to be renewed every five years. That is because circumstances change, the costs of technology go down, and so on. We need to take account of that."[333] As the climate changes, diplomats will need to respond, perhaps driven by demands from the populations of their home countries who become painfully aware of the consequences of climate change.

Five-year cycles of review may arouse continuing opposition. At a G20 pre-meeting in Turkey in November 2015, some countries led by India and Saudi Arabia opposed references to the five-year review process. This opposition carried over into the negotiations in December.[334] Without the five-year reviews, however, it is unlikely that the INDCs can be adjusted to comply with the 2C projections.

Finance became an issue in domestic U.S. politics, leading to questions about future U.S. support for the Paris Agreement. Senators John Barrasso and Jim Inhofe sent Obama a letter warning that "Congress will not be forthcoming" with funding the climate fund unless the Paris Agreement is submitted to the Senate for ratification. Democrats fought to include climate fund money in the 2016 omnibus spending bill. "There are quite a few make-or-break issues in the overall budget bill. This is right up there," said an aide to Sen. Patrick Leahy of Vermont. "The Republicans need Democrats to make it possible to pass this bill, and this is a very high priority for Democrats."[335] If the issue cannot be solved at the domestic level, what are the chances of long-term success of the agreement? Other governments will be watching the U.S. to see if we put our money where our mouth is.

Chapter 6
Global Governance

In this chapter, I offer some personal observations about the issues surrounding negotiations and implementation of climate change agreements. I have been able to observe negotiations, including Conferences of Parties of the UNFCCC and other meetings of climate change experts such as those of the World Meteorological Organization. I have also reported on meetings involving climate change negotiations and discussions.[336]

UN agencies have grown over a period of decades to incorporate more and more functions as governments have requested increased powers and actions from them. From the time that the UN was formed in 1945, it has increased its membership from 51 to 200 countries, each with different but overlapping expectations of its role in the world. Peacekeeping was one of its earliest roles, with the Korean War an early test (facilitated by the absence of USSR diplomats at a crucial meeting). Other functions have grown, particularly in what the UN calls the "Economic and Social Council" that now incorporates UN environmental organizations.

This evolution of the UN has been accompanied by increasing concern on the part of domestic audiences, both for the effects on national sovereignty and the need for global governance.[337] The phrase "global governance" in itself raises strong and sometimes bizarre opposition such as the notion that the UN promotes Satan worship.[338] It tends to arouse emotional responses on the part of politicians, such as Senator James Inhofe (R-OK) who has railed against the UN for encroaching on U.S. national sovereignty for daring to propose that there should be worldwide emissions standards. [339] Denial ideologues in the U.S. have taken the lead in attacking global governance, but there are also denial advocates in countries such as Australia, Canada and the United Kingdom.

Sometimes attacks are crude, as in the myth of "black helicopters" being sent into a country to enforce some drastic policy. These attacks are easily deflected by pointing out that any actions by the UN have to be carried out by members and are not likely to have much effectiveness if they are viewed as hostile to members' interests. A more sophisticated form of attack is doubts about the effectiveness of the UN bodies themselves. "Over more than twenty years, the UNFCCC has made no progress in fulfilling its purpose, instead devolving into a complex process comprised of many moving parts that, from one year to the next, are as likely to move sideways or backward as they are to move forward."[340] This attack relies on the fact that the UN is seldom able to set worldwide standards because of the diverse interests of its member states.

Yet what is the role of the UN in climate negotiations if not to set worldwide standards? Climate change is by nature an international problem. Carbon emitted in any one part of the world affects all other parts of the world. The atmosphere does not respect borders. Even if one nation or group of nations could cease all emissions, other nations could "free ride" and continue to increase emissions without restraint if there were no agreement on standards and enforcement. Such increases would defeat the purposes of reducing emissions by any group of parties as their atmosphere would be almost as badly polluted as it would be had they continued to increase emissions. It was just this fact that undermined action by the U.S. in ratifying the Kyoto Protocol.

It has been the negotiating strategy of the U.S., at least since 2009, to insure that "free riding" by developing countries would not be allowed in the Paris Agreement. When President Obama went to Copenhagen in 2009, he convened the leaders of BASIC (Brazil, South Africa, India and China) countries for informal negotiations on the Copenhagen Accord, which became the basis of the Cancun Agreements to limit temperature increases to 2° C.

There was a lot of grumbling about how this was done, but it became the basis of the negotiations in 2014 and 2015 leading to the Paris Agreement. While the U.S. and other developed countries tended to push worldwide commitments through INDCs, developing countries tried to carve out some exemptions or different commitments through the CBDR principle. These have plagued the negotiations and fed into domestic opposition, particularly in the U.S.

Sovereignty and leadership by strong countries have worked to improve UN governance in some areas, such as peacekeeping, and have worked in other international areas such as trade and finance. But in the case of climate change, the issues are not so amenable to international governance by the UN. While countries can sometimes take domestic measures that enforce UN decisions on carbon emissions, they also need to consider transborder governance issues. Multinational corporations, in particular, can defeat domestic measures by moving production and energy use around.

Forces hostile to global efforts to reduce carbon emissions are strong enough to prevent effective action. This is a result of neo-liberal globalization, which has "…made it easier for more powerful social agents and social institutions to avoid or evade taking responsibility for the consequences of their decisions and actions… This accountability crisis lies at the heart of the failure of global environmental governance."[341] Globalization will be discussed in more detail below, but its role in climate change negotiations is subtle and insidious, as multi-national companies seek ways to evade emissions controls and weaken them through influence on negotiators.

Carbon Budget and Climate Justice

"Carbon Budget" has become a contentious issue in the negotiations, as described in Chapter 5. Scientists have estimated the total amount of carbon that can be emitted to limit global warming the 2C as 1000 gigatons.

This amount can be calculated as a "budget" for allocation among countries that are parties to the UNFCCC. [342] We have already burned about 515 gigatons. For the remaining 485 gigatons, member parties will have to decide how much is available to each.

The Paris Agreement provided for member parties to commit to carbon reductions, but the total amount of these reductions was not sufficient to stay within the carbon budget. (See Chapter 4) As a result, some have said that the Paris Agreement has not effectively addressed the question of budgeting emissions. UNFCCC Executive Secretary Christiana Figueres, referring to the concept of a carbon budget, said "I don't think it's possible. Politically it would be very difficult."[343]

And yet, the morality of climate justice seems to demand a carbon budget. "Today, I see the carbon space occupied by the developed world. We are asking the developed world to vacate the carbon space to accommodate us. That carbon space demand is climate justice," according to Prakash Javadekar, India's environment minister. [344] How the developed world can "vacate the carbon space" is a profound question. While INDCs are a promise to take up less space, "vacating" space is a much more difficult issue. Carbon sequestration is one possibility, but scaling up current technologies is a highly problematic prospect.

Still, there is an outer limit on how much carbon the atmosphere can absorb before climate change gets beyond control. Until UNFCCC member parties agree on an equitable division of that space, there will be a moral vacuity to the negotiations. The Paris Agreement did not address that issue, but only set temperature limits to guide future discussions of allocations and fairness.

A carbon budget would be a game-changer for UNFCCC negotiations. Instead of voluntary pledges of INDCs, member parties would have to fit their emissions into tight limits and would have to calculate how much each country would be allocated. This, in turn, would mean that they would have to commit to limits far below what they currently envision for their home societies. In terms of the negotiations, there would probably be pandemonium as each delegation maneuvered to get more while looking over their shoulders to see if the home government would accept tighter limits. This possibility has led one expert, Michael A. Levi, an energy expert at the Council on Foreign Relations, to say that negotiators "would have all run screaming from the room."[345] Most governments would fight tooth-and-claw against such encroachments on their sovereignty.

However, without a budget, the total amount of emissions permissible to each country cannot be estimated. If countries cannot calculate the limits for their own emissions, how can they set policy to achieve global limits? Large industrialized countries such as the U.S. and Europe, and large emerging economies such as China and India, have used up most of the carbon budget already. Smaller, less industrialized countries see their chances for fossil-fueled development fading as most of the budget is already gone. Bolivia, for example, has complained that the U.S. and other countries are ignoring the limits imposed by such a budget and making it much more difficult for less developed countries to achieve their development goals.[346] They may indeed prevail on the UNFCCC to allocate them higher limits at the expense of developed countries, but only if delegates in future COPs are willing to operate on a foundation of climate justice, an uncertain possibility.

Border Taxes

One area of enforcement that can overcome unfettered market forces is border taxes, which even out the costs for countries that price carbon emissions. These taxes would be levied on products or services that are imported, to match costs incurred by domestic producers when carbon is priced in one country but not in its trading partners. An example would be the EU proposal to charge fees and limit emissions under its cap and trade regime on airlines that fly in and out of Europe. U.S. and Asian airlines met this proposal with strenuous opposition.

116

There are questions about whether such charges would violate rules of the World Trade Organization (WTO), which has provisions against such "restraints" of trade.

Yet without border taxes, the efforts by some (such as the EU) to limit emissions would be defeated by others (such as China) where production of high carbon content goods and services continues unabated. Ironically, the EU benefits from this production when it imports cheaper goods from China but does not account for the carbon content in them.

Border taxes also have a climate justice component, albeit in a less altruistic way. If some countries are willing to fit within a global climate budget while others are not, those who adhere to budgeted limits would "even the score" through border taxes. This would incentivize all member parties to fit into the carbon budget.

Fossil Fuel Reserves

At a more basic level than measuring emissions by product or sector is the issue of fossil fuel reserves. Scientists have gathered more and more evidence that indicates that about four-fifths, or 80%, of fossil fuels must remain in the ground.[347] So enforcement agencies must decide how to slow and eventually stop production and use of oil, gas and coal. This will encounter huge resistance as fossil fuel companies come to realize how drastically it affects their assets. At present, these companies are spending more than $600 billion a year to develop new fields for production when they should be shutting down production on an orderly basis. Who will decide which facilities should be shut down?[348]

Of course, it will make little sense to shut down facilities rapidly unless there are alternative energy sources ready to replace them, also on an orderly basis. This, too, is an issue of global governance since most fossil fuel companies are multinationals and controls in one country will not be effective unless matched by controls in all countries. If all parties could agree on

117

shutdowns, some financial and trade measures could be carried out through existing institutions such as WTO.

During the negotiations on the implementation of the Kyoto Protocol, these issues were raised but not resolved. The main approach of diplomats was to set targets for emissions reductions and let domestic governments find ways to enforce them. There were provisions for MRV – Measuring, Reporting and Verification – to insure that the parties to the protocol met their commitments. Some of these provisions carried over to the negotiations for the Paris Agreement, but enforcement so far has been weak and there is no assurance that it will be any stronger under the new regime.

Fossil fuel companies in Europe have recognized that they cannot utilize all of their reserves. They called on negotiators to make an effective Paris Agreement that puts a price on fossil fuels.[349] Even OPEC (Organization of Petroleum Exporting Countries) said that is members should be "actively and positively engaged" in the Paris climate negotiations and agreed "climate change, environmental protection and sustainable development are a major concern for us all."[350] Noticeably absent from the list of companies that support an agreement were U.S. oil companies Exxon-Mobil and Chevron. "I've never had a customer come to me and ask to pay a higher price for oil, gas or other products," said Chevron CEO John S. Watson.[351] Exxon-Mobil has aroused the fury of two congress members, who want it investigated for climate change denial. "ExxonMobil's apparent behavior is similar to cigarette companies that repeatedly denied harm from tobacco and spread uncertainty and misinformation to the public," Ted Lieu and Mark DeSaulnier, both Democratic members of Congress from California, wrote. "We ask that the DoJ [Department of Justice] similarly investigate Exxon for organizing a sustained deception campaign disputing climate science and failing to disclose truthful information to investors and the public."[352] Exxon-Mobil has been working for decades to stave off the inevitable downgrading of its assets by denying climate science. Until all fossil fuel companies realize that they cannot continue to extract all of the oil in their identified reserves, the problem of rising emissions will persist.

Enforcement

Enforcement will be particularly complex under a new regime that includes all 194 member parties, rather than just the dozen or so parties in Annex I of the Kyoto Protocol.[353] Negotiations on enforcement were the most protracted and contentious of all the issues, which is why many countries wanted to avoid them through voluntary commitments.

Even with the voluntary nature of the Paris Agreement, there is a mechanism for enforcement. EU climate commissioner, Miguel Cañete, said "We have to assess globally how the INDCs have been implemented. If there is additional financial support available, those who have made conditional pledges, we will have to look at them and see how we target financial support."[354] The EU has been one of the parties insisting on a legally binding agreement, and although it has not succeeded in incorporating legally-binding provisions in the Paris Agreement, it has used financing as an enforcement tool.

International negotiations proceed at glacial speed – indeed the glaciers are melting faster than the world can agree on climate action. Sometimes smaller jurisdictions can proceed faster. According to Frank Biermann, "There is no doubt that engagement of cities, civil society, and the private sector is urgently needed. Earth system governance cannot be addressed by governments alone. It must include all societal actors and individual citizens. For one, technology change and effective policies at local and national levels need to become a driving force of progress."[355] States such as the New England states, with their Regional Greenhouse Gas Initiative; California, with Cap and Trade, and provinces such as Quebec and British Columbia, are proceeding without waiting for their federal governments. U.S. cities, led by Seattle, San Francisco and others of the city federation called U.S. Conference of Mayors Climate Protection Agreement, have initiated climate action. Seattle relies mainly on renewable power and offers citizens an option to buy into solar power projects that then return credits on their electric bills as the projects pay off.

One issue that colors negotiations on climate change is globalization. Climate change is of course a global issue and must be resolved through global efforts. Globalization of business, particularly finance and production, has opened up possibilities for enforcing emissions reductions through financial and corporate institutions. On the other hand, globalization could hamper enforcement by bypassing national authorities and moving production to areas with low enforcement of environmental regulations. This has often been the case, as noted by some critics: "They point to the uncanny correlation between the globalization of trade, investment, production, and consumption, on the one hand, and the globalization of environmental problems, on the other. When economic globalization accelerates, they point out, so do resource depletion, deforestation, species extinction, pollution, and greenhouse gas emissions. When globalization slows as a result of a global recession, so do these rates of ecological degradation."[356]

While globalization has been pursued heedless of climate change and other environmental problems, it could be reoriented toward international cooperation on resolving environmental problems. Proper incentives are needed, but these will come only from the political sector, not the economic sector. Carbon taxes and other means of properly pricing energy will provide these incentives if targeted at phasing out fossil fuels quickly.

Trade agreements have different effects on enforcement, depending on how they are drafted. When they use provisions that do not enforce the highest environmental standards of every party, those parties with lower standards can attract companies seeking to avoid

120

the higher standards. There are also provisions in some agreements such as NAFTA (North American Free Trade Agreement) and the Trans-Pacific Partnership called "investor-state dispute settlement" that permit lawsuits by companies against governments that they deem too restrictive. These provisions can also undermine enforcement of carbon limits it they are deemed harmful to profits.

There is no reason that trade agreements must undermine environmental standards or enforcement of emissions limits. Indeed, they could have the opposite effect by enabling governments and businesses to uphold higher standards through border taxes and other provisions to "even out" the true costs of energy use. If provisions of the Paris Agreement are to be enforced at the international level, this function of trade agreements must be written into their texts. Since no nation would agree to cede sovereignty to a global government, it is necessary for parties to the agreements at lower levels to exercise their separate sovereignties in reaching and maintaining the highest standards.

Climate change is a "wicked" problem because of all of the complications of agreeing and enforcing standards that would stabilize the climate. Its wickedness is captured in the economic analysis of "externalities" that infuse the problem: "...externalization of environmental risks across space and time has become so routine, and is likely to continue in the absence of a significant transformation of social structures and social relationships. Climate change provides an exemplary illustration of this problem, since it is not clearly visible or palpable to many constituencies: the cause-and-effect relationships are complex, uncertain, and not well understood by laypeople; there exists political disputation by climate deniers over whether climate change is traceable to human activity; the problem is largely irreversible across human timescales; and while the longer-term benefits of action are widely recognized, many states and key constituencies fiercely resist the short-term costs that would flow from concerted regulation."[357]

Externalities "across space and time" are particularly hard to measure, as so many disputes about the models used in climate science indicate.[358] Projections of climate change in the future and its effects on different localities are couched in probabilities, and scientists will admit that they do not have all of the details exactly right. But the overall effect and its probable course are clear enough, and they show a wicked tendency to affect different places and generations in dramatically different ways. We in the temperate North, with its moderate weather and somewhat regular rainfall, have been fortunate to have a stable climate and food security. Our descendants, and those in less favorable locations, will suffer the consequences of our actions much more than we seem to understand.

What will be necessary for these considerations to come into the global dialog and, eventually, decision-making at the global level? Unfortunately, the usual answer to this question is a major crisis, perhaps with extensive damage and death. We have had a number of previews in the forms of droughts and extreme weather,[359] but none has completely changed the way that we make decisions. Fossil fuel use continues to grow, emissions are increasing, and governments are equivocating on the extent of economic changes needed.

What forms will these crises take? Africa offers some examples.

Africans are expected to be the worst hit by climate change, suffering worsening droughts that will directly reduce food availability. Whether you believe it is relevant or not – and most people I speak to think it is – Africans have contributed the least to climate change, belonging to the only continent bar Antarctica that has not yet significantly industrialised (indeed, many parts have been deindustrialising since

122

the 1980s). In the Anthropocene, deaths from climate change will not be caused by the weather per se (apart from a tiny percentage of cases), but rather by the fatal synergy between climate change and a catalogue of other misfortunes: natural disasters such as locust plagues; fake seeds; low productivity due to poor health; poor governance and corruption (that sees, for example, much of the agricultural budget vanish); social and gender inequalities; poor infrastructure; and trade laws and protectionist agreements that favour rich countries.[360]

Chapter 7
Sabotaging the Planet

Agreements on environmental issues are not simple or easy for diplomats to negotiate. They are even more difficult for some politicians to accept, as we will see shortly. Regardless of the difficulties, however, there have been successful agreements on international environmental issues.

Many people have suggested that an agreement on climate would be similar to an already successful agreement on ozone, the Montreal Protocol to the Vienna Convention for the Protection of the Ozone Layer. The Montreal Protocol, negotiated in 1987 and successfully implemented in the 28 years since then, has drastically reduced ozone depleting substances in the atmosphere while enabling many countries to develop substitutes for use in refrigeration, air conditioning and other uses of chlorofluorocarbons, the principal ozone-depleting substances (ODS).

There are still problems with the Montreal Protocol, but it is often cited as an example of an atmospheric pollution agreement that combined the efforts of many member parties in a cooperative effort to solve an international environmental challenge. Why not transfer some of the key ingredients to the UNFCCC? As noted by some scholars, there are indeed similar parts to each but also crucial differences:

> While both regimes establish targets and timetables, in the ozone regime, all industrialized countries must meet essentially the same standards, while in the climate regime, different industrialized countries have very different targets for reducing emissions. Developing countries accepted binding controls to reduce the use of ODS under the Montreal Protocol, but there are no binding commitments on developing

countries to reduce GHG emissions under the Kyoto Protocol. Finally, governments have expanded and strengthened the ozone regime, primarily because of scientific consensus and the availability of substitutes for ozone-depleting chemicals. In contrast, while the IPCC has provided the scientific consensus that climate change is occurring, many governments have refused to take significant action, in part because of concerns for the short-terms cost associated with reducing the use of coal, oil, and natural gas – fossil fuels that contribute most to CO_2 emissions.[361]

As noted, *many governments have refused to take significant action,* because of *"concerns"* that are often expressed by domestic political opposition that develops from denial. In this chapter, we will examine the sources and effects of that denial.[362]

One other aspect of the Montreal Protocol that differs from the UNFCCC, the Kyoto Protocol and the Paris Agreement is that climate change has polarized parties.

> The framers of the treaty on ozone hoped to help history repeat itself concerning CO_2. But history does not repeat itself. History informs the contexts in which events unfold and thus prevents its own repetition. The relationship between ozone and climate change is a case in point. During negotiations over a potential global warming treaty, opponents were able to take the initiative in part because of their experiences with the ozone debate. The success in regulating CFCs put powerful corporate and governmental bodies on notice... Opponents of regulation of greenhouse gases consequently were able to carve out their own niches alongside environmental

NGOs in the negotiation process, which tipped the strategic playing field on climate change in their favor. [363]

Because of the stakes involved – industrial production and transportation on a large scale, freedom of movement, lifestyle – the corporations and politicians are using opportunities presented by the slow pace of negotiations to oppose effective emissions reductions.

No politician will admit to sabotaging the planet. The justifications used by many politicians to avoid action are based on the problem that all of them face – that reelection depends on meeting expectations of the electorate. Nevertheless, politicians do have the principal responsibilities for deciding on carbon limits and carrying out policies to realize this objective. No one can escape the responsibility for preventing "dangerous anthropogenic interference with the climate system" as the UNFCC convention text states. All of us are responsible to one degree or another, but politicians have a special responsibility as decision-makers.

Many politicians have attempted to avoid responsibility by changing the subject. Two stratagems are used: (1) *"I'm not a scientist,"* and (2) *"jobs, jobs, jobs."*[364]

- Justification #1 is a cop-out by politicians who know better – they don't need scientific credentials to understand the problem. The science is clear – and has been explained many times to the politicians who are willing to hear – and any doubts that politicians nurture are based on pseudo-science. Basing policy on pseudo-science is sabotaging the planet.

- Justification #2 is based on a false dichotomy between climate action and jobs. In fact, effective climate action can enhance job growth if done right – with renewable energy and efficiency, for example. [365] If by

126

"defending jobs" a politician means locking in fossil fuel energy in a sector of the economy, regardless of how damaging its effects on the environment or employment, that is sabotaging the planet.

When policymakers decide that they do not want to use these stratagems to sabotage the planet, they will have to initiate climate policy based on international agreements. One country or group of countries cannot prevent sabotage of the planet alone – although the EU has tried mightily to do so. While the UN is not a perfect organization by any stretch of the imagination, it is the only one we've got when it comes to international climate policies.

Multilateral Agreements

Multilateral environment agreements have become one of the UN's most active area of negotiations. Many trace their provenance to the 1972 Stockholm Conference on the Human Environment. The secretary-general of that conference, the late Maurice Strong, viewed environmental agreements as the epitome of multilateral or global governance. "The entire global system on which all life depends must inevitably and inexorably lead us back to a new kind of globalism."[366] The issue of global governance is one that arouses considerable animus from denial ideologues.[367]

An issue that sometimes plagues international negotiations is the scope of multilateral agreements. UNFCCC decisions are by definition multilateral, since the organization itself encompasses virtually all members of the UN. Some have suggested that negotiations on climate change would be more effective if they involved fewer countries, as for example the "G20" group of countries.[368] Observers have noted that this is not likely to be effective for climate change.

At the global level of earth system governance, there are hardly any promising alternatives to multilateral institutions and negotiations. "Minilateralism" is unlikely to achieve the much-needed legitimacy among countries that are not invited to participate. The long-term effectiveness of solutions agreed upon at Group of 8 or Group of 20 meetings is open to debate, especially when it comes to broad questions of sustainability governance. More than 150 countries are not represented in the Group of 20.[369]

There is no alternative to the UN when it comes to climate change negotiations. All countries in the world contribute to the problem of carbon emissions, and all will suffer the consequences of the failure to control emissions. Nevertheless, there are vicious attacks on the UN, particularly when it comes to climate negotiations.

Because some have despaired of reaching an agreement through the UN, there are suggestions that nations impose unilateral measures such as carbon taxes and then use border taxes to equalize costs for domestic manufacturers vs. foreign manufacturers. This kind of approach has been described as follows:

> If agreements cannot be reached, it may be possible to internationalize the economic costs of strong climate policies by imposing unilateral border adjustments. Where production costs are raised by the introduction of a carbon tax, for example, importers could be required to pay a tax on the carbon content of imports except where the exporting country imposes a similar tax. At the same time the carbon tax would be refunded on exports, removing their competitive disadvantage on foreign markets.[370]

Such unilateral actions are fraught with risks, however. WTO (World Trade Organization) rules may be used to impose sanctions on those countries that use border taxes or other means to equalize carbon costs. The WTO Committee on Trade and Environment debates these rules and may provide some exceptions, but the WTO Dispute Settlement Body can impose sanctions if border taxes or other climate measures are deemed anti-trade.

One of the most destructive ways that denial ideologues seek to sabotage the planet is vicious attacks on the UN, using reasoning far removed from reality.[371] These attacks undermine social support at the domestic level for the decisions of the UNFCCC COPs, and give politicians license to ignore needed changes in economic and energy systems.

Strobe Talbott, Deputy Secretary of State from 1994 to 2001, makes a serious indictment of the role of the U.S. in its part of the negotiation process.

> The United States is a case in point. Some of the best climate scientists in the world are Americans. So are some of the most eloquent and influential advocates for a global compact. Moreover, global compacts are an American specialty. At pivotal moments in the twentieth century, U.S. presidents were the chief architects, master-builders, and principal funders of international institutions – notably, the UN itself – that constitute a rule-based world order and have promoted the prosperity and security now threatened by climate change.[372]

Talbott praises the U.S. for its role in founding the UN, and notes that the "rule-based world" is threatened by climate change. While not spelling that out, Talbott may have in mind that climate change has contributed to serious conflicts around the world. He goes on to lament the problem of U.S. politicians who are unable to see the need for UN action on climate change.

> Yet in the face of that threat, all four of America's most recent

presidents…have, for one reason or another, been unable to rise fully to the challenge. Part of the reason is domestic politics. The nation's chief executive shares responsibility for success and failure with his partners in government at the other end of Pennsylvania Avenue, on Capitol Hill. Beyond the frictions between the two major political parties and the two branches of government, there has been another, more basic impediment: the difficulty of reconciling the diplomatic ideal of a globally binding treaty with the political reality of national sovereignty and economic self-interest.[373]

Talbott has put his finger on one of the crucial issues of multilateral environment agreements: *"the difficulty of reconciling the diplomatic ideal of a globally binding treaty with the political reality of national sovereignty and economic self-interest."* As member parties look at the ideals embodied in the UNFCCC preamble, which makes addressing climate change "a common concern of humankind," they see the need for ambitious actions. But when diplomats return to their home capitals, they face the "political reality" of economic special interests who sponsor vicious attacks on the international system.

Politicians reflect these vicious attacks and practice climate change denial. Senator James Inhofe (R-OK), for example, has said "Climate is changing and climate has always changed and always will. The hoax is that there are some people who are so arrogant to think they are so powerful they can change climate. Man can't change climate."[374] By claiming that *"man can't change climate,"* Inhofe is denying human influences in a pseudo-scientific way that has no basis in fact, but is based entirely on belief. In fact, Inhofe bases his pseudo-science on faith: "My point is, God's still up there. The arrogance of people to think that we human beings would be able to change what he is doing in the climate is to me outrageous."[375] This misuse of religion is a corruption of faith. The statement that *"God's still up there"* is a religious belief, while the statement that *"human beings would [not] be able to change what he is doing in the climate"* is an ideological statement subject to scientific refutation.

What is the pseudo-science that politicians use to sabotage the planet? As we have seen in Chapter 2, the claim that the *"globe is cooling"* is a false claim often used by denial ideologues to deny climate science. Politicians pick up on this claim and do not bother to test it against the data that shows that the four warmest years on record are 2015, 2014, 2010 and 2005. So much for a cooling planet.

What are the jobs that politicians are trying to protect? Many, such as Senate Majority Leader Mitch McConnell, speak of a "war on coal."[376] This is a sector of the economy that has undergone tremendous job decline without any regulations on carbon emissions before 2015. Thankfully, the underground mining of coal has virtually ceased while coal companies use much safer methods. Many jobs have been lost through changes in mining practices unrelated to climate change. Unfortunately, methods such as mountaintop removal and open-pit mining are highly destructive. The "war on coal" is not really a destruction of jobs; it is a battle against environmentally destructive practices. Coupled with the high ratio of carbon emissions to energy produced, coal is one of the most devastating sources of energy used today. Phasing it out is one of the most important policies required for climate stability.

These are not just economic or political arguments. Economists have debated the costs and benefits of climate policies for years (cf. Nordhaus and Stern) and politicians have found ways to avoid issues raised by climate change. The argument now is what moral principles apply to climate change. If one argues, for example, that current populations have higher priority than future populations, one might say that climate policies should not entail high costs for people now alive. If one argues that wealthy populations have higher priorities than poor populations because they have "earned" the right to their lifestyles, then one can say that climate policies should not entail any redistribution of income, as many denial ideologues have argued.[377]

Both of these arguments are morally bankrupt, however. You would seldom hear any politician say, "Let's swindle our grandchildren" or "Let's destroy the earth." No one can explicitly justify shortchanging children and grandchildren to support comfortable lifestyles of current generations. No one would argue against survival of the planet's ecosystems. Everyone benefits from ecosystem services, rich and poor.

Compounding the ethical problems of international disparities are domestic problems that sabotage the negotiations. There is a failure of will that stems from the domestic pressures that bind the delegates. "This failure reflects philosophical and ideological differences between negotiators about the nature and extent of historical and future responsibility for global warming, imbalances in negotiating power between the most responsible and the most vulnerable parties, and the shallow understanding of and ethical commitment to international responsibility evident in the political culture of most developed nations." [378] The *"ideological differences"* come from domestic pressure groups such as the denial movement in the U.S. When the political culture of member parties does not support understanding of or ethical commitment to steps necessary to prevent climate disruption, the delegates will not have incentives to reach agreement at the level necessary to mitigate climate change.

Whether or not morally bankrupt arguments rise to the level of conscious decisions is the key question. One of the more frustrating aspects of climate change morality is the suppression, conscious or unconscious, of moral sensibility. Many people simply do not want to face the facts. It will take vociferous activism by those of

132

us who want to face facts, and do something, to bring these morally bankrupt arguments to the surface and deal with them.

One might ask, if science indicates action and governments agree on measures that might mitigate climate change, why do societies continue to resist needed changes? Many obstacles are encountered in the implementation of climate change agreements, but they essentially come down to short-term versus long-term interests. Climate change often becomes a low priority because of more immediate economic and political concerns.

Significant obstacles remain to implementing solutions, however, in part because concern for environmental issues remains relatively low compared to other economic or political interests. The effectiveness of, and compliance with, international environmental regimes likely cannot increase significantly until public officials raise the priority of these issues or until elevated public concern and concerted individual action forces them to do so.[379]

How do citizens raise priorities for public officials, if not through concerted action? Politicians do respond to pressure, and most of the strongest pressures have been in the direction of increased use of fossil fuels to sustain growth. As the credibility of denial ideology fades,[380] and weather events become more worrisome for the public, *"elevated public concern"* will become an increasingly effective.

Consumption

At an even more basic level, the issue of consumption and lifestyles arises in the context of climate change negotiations. As noted in Chapter 3, developing countries "identify the high levels of consumption in industrialized countries as a key cause of global environmental degradation."[381] During negotiations of the

133

Paris Agreement, there were suggestions by some developing countries to include text in the preamble on "sustainable lifestyles and sustainable patterns of consumption," and "the importance of promoting social and economic development."[382]

Because American, European and other advanced economies are based on cheap energy, climate action seems to be an existential threat to those societies. As long as they continue along the path of increasing fossil fuel consumption, they tend to sabotage climate stabilization actions needed to meet the crisis. Until they get away from fossil fuels, these societies risk increasing damage to their economies from the consequences of climate change. Their credibility in the negotiations, particularly in enlisting the participation of developing countries in emissions reductions, depends on advanced economic systems reorienting energy use away from fossil fuels. But the growth model used by advanced economy depends on increased energy inputs, and phasing out fossil fuels will require major structural changes.

These changes will require shifting resources in a way that creates winners (such as renewable energy industries) and losers (such as fossil fuel industries). By some accounts such a shift would cost economies up to $1 trillion dollars a year. Bjorn Lomborg, President of the Copenhagen Consensus Center, stated his objection to the Paris Agreement as follows:

> The cuts on the table in Paris, then, will leave the global economy, in rough terms, $1 trillion short every year for the rest of the century – and that's if the politicians do everything right. If not, the real cost could double. All of these high-flown promises will fail to accomplish anything substantial to rein in climate change. At best, the emissions cuts pledged in Paris will prevent a total temperature rise by 2100 of only 0.306 degrees Fahrenheit, according to a peer-

reviewed study I recently published in Global Policy.[383]

This sort of one-sided economic analysis assumes that cuts in emissions are only a cost, not a benefit. The supposedly miniscule reduction in temperatures comes from a model that projects only a few current INDC pledges, not the possibility of more ambitious pledges in the future. It ignores the economic benefits of investment in renewable energies. Nevertheless, faulty reasoning such as this has been the basis of denial attempts to sabotage the Paris Agreement.

At its basic level, the growth model uses assumptions about nature that are faulty. In the terms of environmental economics, nature is a "primary economy" that provides resources and ecological services for the human economy, which is a secondary economy. In the modern world, a tertiary economy has developed that abstracts value from land, labor and capital (the basic elements of the secondary economy). This value then becomes the basis of the model of growth, but it is remote from the basic resources and services of nature. As a result, growth models overlook the costs of using up resources such as the carrying capacity of the atmosphere for carbon concentrations. While this carrying capacity seems like an abstract invisible thing – carbon dioxide is, after all, an odorless and transparent gas – it is nevertheless real and severely consequential phenomenon. Economists ignore this at their and our peril. As John Greer noted in *The Wealth of Nature:*

> The primary economy of Nature, the base of the entire structure, is ignored by most contemporary economists, and has essentially no place in the economic policy of today's industrial nations. The assumption hardwired into nearly all modern thought is that the economic contributions of the primary economy will always be there so long as the secondary and tertiary economy are working as they should. This may just be

135

the Achilles' heel of the entire structure, because it means that mismatches between the primary economy and the other two economies not only won't be addressed — they won't even be noticed.[384]

Economic growth has enabled societies to rise beyond the limits on health and well-being that made life in "ancient" societies "nasty, brutish and short," to use Hobbe's notable phrase. While these more primitive societies suffered high rates of disease and starvation, they had less impact on the environment. Brooke describes this conundrum as follows:

> Ancient populations suffered poor individual life outcomes, with poor health and low life expectancy; conversely, they imposed relatively low environmental impact and enjoyed long-term societal sustainability. Whatever their flaws, and there were many, ancient societies should not be condemned for any major environmental failings. Modern populations, by contrast, enjoy excellent and improving high individual outcomes, with amazingly good health and high life expectancy, and are causing systemic changes on the entire global ecology. Whether they are sustainable is very much an open question.[385]

As consumers of fossil fuel energy, we do enjoy more healthy lives and a rich diet. Whether our lifestyles can be sustained is a dubious proposition, but there are plenty of reasons that denial ideologues fear the consequences of climate action. Badly managed, a panic reaction to climate consequences will lead to rapid decline in living standards. Similarly, continued denial will lead to an even faster decline at some inflection point. Only a well-managed "soft landing" will overcome the problems of the current climate trends while making healthy lifestyles sustainable. This makes many politicians fearful of abandoning the current model of economic growth because they lack understanding the need for a soft landing.

Traditional models of economic growth are a major part of problems caused by consumerism; "consumerism is a danger to the planet."[386] This danger comes from the tendency to view all growth as dependent on fossil-fueled increases in wealth, not as improvement in the quality of life that can be sustained without ruining the planet.

While business as usual continues, people's expectations are unrealistically maintained at a high and growing level of consumption. "The accelerating drawdown of fossil fuels over the last three centuries shifted the process into overdrive, allowing the minority of the Earth's population who lived in Europe or the more privileged nations of the European diaspora — the United States first among them — not only to adopt what were, by the standards of all other human societies, extravagantly lavish lifestyles, but to expect that those lifestyles would become even more lavish in the future."[387] Whether these expectations can be satisfied without climate catastrophe is one of the key questions facing world leaders.

Some of the psychology of consumption comes from the perception of status based on luxury products and services. When inequality in society is high, conspicuous consumption (to borrow Veblen's term) requires the intensive use of fossil fuels. Luxury products, international travel, inefficient large homes and luxury cars all result in higher carbon emissions. Some commentators on the immorality of inequality have linked it to climate change.

> If, to cut carbon emissions, we need to limit economic growth severely in the rich countries, then it is important to know that this does not mean sacrificing improvements in the real quality of life – in the quality of life as measured by health, happiness, friendship and community life,

which really matters. However, rather than simply having fewer of all the luxuries which substitute for and prevent us recognizing our more fundamental needs, inequality has to be reduced simultaneously. We need to create more equal societies able to meet our real social needs. Instead of policies to deal with global warming being experienced simply as imposing limits on the possibilities of material satisfaction, they need to be coupled with egalitarian policies which steer us to new and more fundamental ways of improving the quality of our lives.[388]

Emphasis on fossil-fueled economic growth in member parties is particularly destructive to negotiations of an effective climate agreement. "Catch-up industrialization in the emerging economies, insatiable energy hunger in the countries that industrialized early, and the worldwide spread of a social model geared to growth and resource consumption make it seem unrealistic that further warming by mid-century will be kept at or below 2[C]."[389] The "social model" that controls energy use in most countries depends on unlimited use of resources, but resources, especially the capacity of the atmosphere to absorb carbon, are not unlimited.

It is not only in developing countries that energy use and development seem to conflict with resolution of the climate crisis. Maija Lukin, the mayor of Kotzebue, Alaska, said "It's a double-edged sword for us, because we know that the industry does help to create climate change, but we understand that it's going to do that anyway, and if it has to happen, we want our people to benefit from that development."[390] Lukin was referring to the oil industry, whose investment in Arctic communities has benefitted residents. Kotzebue is an Arctic community where rapid warming of the Arctic has created problems with the infrastructure and traditional livelihood of the community. When Native American residents look at the effects of climate change, they see problems looming but they also want benefits of economic growth. Kotzebue residents use trucks and snowmobiles to get around while their traditional hunting and fishing grounds are disappearing.

Consumption in developed countries is based almost entirely in rapid use of fossil fuels. "The accelerating drawdown of fossil fuels over the last three centuries shifted the process into overdrive, allowing the minority of the Earth's population who lived in Europe or the more privileged nations of the European diaspora – the United States first among them – not only to adopt what were, by the standards of all other human societies, extravagantly lavish lifestyles, but to expect that those lifestyles would become even more lavish in the future."[391] These expectations will be sorely tested in the coming decades as the use of fossil fuels becomes more and more problematic.

Achieving the understanding of economic growth without fossil fuels is fraught with conceptual difficulties. Some have argued that the result of regulation of greenhouse gases by EPA (Chapter 2) would be deindustrialization of the U.S.:

> The obvious result would be a mandate for the deindustrialization of the US since the US economy is dependent on the use of inexpensive and reliable energy. The economic effects of such an outcome would be literally catastrophic to the US economy and population. The only likely ways to avoid such an outcome would be EPA withdrawal of its Endangerment Finding...[392]

Such an argument raises the specter of poverty for the population, forced on it by greenhouse gas regulations. This is a typical scare tactic of denial ideology in opposing climate policies. Nevertheless, it must be overcome with more positive views of growth based on sustainable use of resources.

World leaders have recognized the conundrum of consumption and fossil fuel energy dependence. In his encyclical (see Chapter 3), Pope Francis stated "Humanity is called to recognize the need for changes of lifestyle, production and consumption, in order to combat this warming or at least the human causes which produce or aggravate it." [393] Pope Francis makes clear the relationship between climate change and consumption. "However, many of [the negative impacts of climate change] indicate that such effects will continue to worsen if we continue with current models of production and consumption."[394] The encyclical is not a socialist diatribe against capitalism, but a religious teaching document aimed and changing the moral approach of societies to climate change. It is particularly addressed to the immorality of inequality between classes in societies and between developed and developing countries.

Consumption is an issue not only because of inequalities between developed and developing countries, but also because of the fear of many in high-consumption societies that they will be reduced to poverty if an international agreement such as UNFCCC mandates changes in energy use. While this fear is ill founded, it holds sway in denial ideology.[395] It is constantly used as a justification for resisting climate action and is implicit in the opposition to binding commitments under the UNFCCC, which are viewed as expressions of world government, a nemesis of denial ideology. [396] When domestic opposition undermines the diplomats who are trying to resolve the climate crisis, negotiations are sabotaged for the sake of a false ideology.

Delegates must also face the issue of allocation of emissions reductions in terms of the competition for remaining "air space."

Scientists tell us that we have space for about 1,000 billion tonnes of CO2 equivalent (CO2e) in our atmosphere if we

140

are to have a reasonable chance of limiting average global temperature increase to 2°C. From around the year 1800 to date, we have emitted more than 500 billion tonnes of CO2 and the equivalent of about 200 billion tonnes of CO2e in the form of other gases and pollutants. We currently emit around 10 billion tonnes of CO2e per annum so at the current rate, we will fill the available space within the next 25 to 30 years. In other words, there is space for about 300 billion tonnes of CO2 up for grab by all of the world's nations, and they have been invited by the UN Climate Talks to state how much they want to grab.[397]

While somewhat harsh, this analysis highlights one of the principal problems with climate negotiations: member parties are in competition for the best "deal" for their own populations. This competition underlies the contentious CBDR (common but differentiated responsibilities) issues that have stalked the negotiations from the beginning – developing countries want a better "deal" since they need the air space for increased emissions as their poor citizens become richer consumers. Developed countries want to keep their living standards high, so they are unwilling to cede much "air space."

In relation to consumption patterns, there is an additional problem for negotiators: trade barriers. One proposal for reduction of carbon emissions is carbon footprint labeling, the concept that any product on the market can be measured for carbon use in its production and transportation. This proposal has some risks in terms of international trade law, however.

Current discussions on environmental standards and certification requirements are also focusing on carbon footprint labeling, which show the quantity of carbon-dioxide emissions associated with making and transporting products. While the EU largely supports such carbon accounting efforts, developing countries fear that such schemes could be used as trade restrictions in disguise and impose burdensome and costly requirements, thus impeding their access to important export markets. There is also concern about the methodology for determining carbon footprints, in terms of both accuracy and consistency, and that carbon footprint certificates were mostly being awarded to agricultural products, fish, and raw materials, which have a greater impact on developing countries.[398]

The methodology of determining carbon footprints is still limited in its capability to accurately measure carbon emission effects, for example, of importing fresh fruits and other foodstuffs. There are even more perverse effects of globalization of food production.

For example, the ready availability of every vegetable or fruit in your supermarket throughout the year is partly the result of a shift from subsistence farming in parts of many developing countries to intensive cash cropping, the wages and profits of which do not translate into sufficient food and social development in many local societies. In addition to the environmental externalities of flying these products to northern markets, cash crops bring questionable benefits to developing countries. Agribusinesses, not farmers, often reap the benefits and own the best-quality land. Chemical fertilizers and pesticides are relied on to produce uniform, export-quality produce; far fewer of these chemicals were needed to grow local and subsistence crops.[399]

Citizens concerned about their carbon footprints need to keep these considerations in mind. Carbon footprint analysis is a useful way for consumers to measure their own effect on climate change. There are a number of web sites that permit consumers to measure their own footprints,[400] but they do not have precise measurements for consumption of different products, only a general calculation of consumption. The best do have options for distinguishing between local and imported foods, for example, but do not list particular foods that might have higher or lower emissions in their production and transportation.

It would be much more meaningful to have food and other consumer products labeled with emissions. If ecolabeling of products by carbon emissions used in their production and transportation were to become acceptable, it would permit consumers to reduce their emissions by selective buying.

Of course, no matter how many people calculate their carbon footprints, the increase in emissions will not subside until alternative energy is widely adopted. That will require pressure from people who understand the issues and the political levers that are required to move societies away from fossil fuels. Building communities of concerned citizens is one of the major challenges of those of us who are aware of the effects of climate change and want to change the current trajectory of major economies of the world.

Divestment

Another area of moral concern is investment in fossil fuels. The advocacy group 350.org has been recommending that churches as well as other institutions divest their holdings of fossil fuel company equities. This has generated some controversy as some churches disagree (e.g., the Church of England with more than 150 million pounds invested in Shell and BP), and argue that they can influence decisions by remaining invested in the companies.

One church group which is planning divestment to make a statement is the World Council of Churches, based in Geneva, Switzerland.

The World Council of Churches, which represents around 560m Christians in 140 countries, has adopted a divestment strategy for its 16.7 million Swiss franc investment portfolio. Its finance policy committee decided in July that fossil fuels should be added to the list of sectors in which the council would not invest. "The use of fossil fuels must be significantly reduced and by not investing in those companies we want to show a direction we need to follow as a human family to address climate changes properly," said Rev Dr. Olav Fykse Tveit, WCC general secretary.[401]

Whether the WCC example is followed in member denominations depends on their governance, since the WCC is only a confederation of churches that join voluntarily. Nevertheless, WCC does carry some moral authority and could influence denominations in various countries to divest. The question is what wider influence this moral authority portends. Individual churches have taken positions on climate change but the national church organizations sometimes lag behind. The national church organizations are more likely to have sway over national governments. They should support the approach of the UNFCCC.

A spokesman for the UNFCCC secretariat, Nick Nuttall, said "We support divestment as it sends a signal to companies, especially coal companies, that the age of 'burn what you like, when you like' cannot continue."[402] As a signal, divestment seems to be innocuous but it does seem to have stirred up a hornet's nest. Benjamin Sporton, acting chief executive of the World Coal Association, responded "The coal divestment campaign is not comparable to any other divestment campaign. Active and responsible investors play a vital role in encouraging investment in cleaner coal technologies. Demand for coal is not going away."[403] He seems to believe that coal-powered energy can continue an only needs "cleaner coal technologies," an oxymoron.

Other fossil fuel companies are not so sanguine about the future of their industry. A number of oil company executives have started to grapple with the issue of climate change and its implications for the future of their investments in petroleum reserves. They have even begun to pay attention to churches, especially the Catholic Church.[404] When the large energy corporations and churches team up to address climate change, who could continue to deny the science? Unfortunately, there are many.

Like many of the proposals to address climate change, divestment has drawn the ire of denial ideologues. One of the leading denial organizations is Heartland Institute, and here is what a blog at heartland.org said about Bill McKibben's campaign for divestment:

> McKibben gets the credit for starting the Divest-Invest movement, largely because of his scary articles in Rolling Stone and Grist. But McKibben is the sock puppet in this fight and has secured only 13 commitments to divest, all from small colleges with small endowments. He doesn't have traction in the trustee councils of big universities, which refuse to give any symbolic divestment pledge because they have a legal fiduciary trust to keep their institutions solvent.[405]

Using the conspiracy theory approach that denial ideologues are fond of, the statement suggests that McKibben is a front for the Wallace Global Fund II, and intimates that its rationale is radical. It suggests that the Fund has an "ideological goal of eliminating coal use."

> The current heirs, co-chairmen Scott and Randall Wallace and treasurer Christy Wallace, along with executive director Ellen

Dorsey (2012 compensation, $298,596), realized their investments in coal companies conflicted with their ideological goal of eliminating coal use and divested the offending securities, according to the fund's website. It was a short step to building their example into a movement.[406]

Bill McKibben would probably be surprised to learn that his movement is built from the example of the Wallace Global Fund. As a grass-roots movement, 350.org is a long way from the top-down model used by denial ideologues such as Heartland and Americans for Prosperity.[407]

Environmental Law

Ultimately, diplomats negotiate environmental law. "Environmental law's primary function seeks to bring society into compliance with natural laws, which, in the end, determine whether citizens prosper or perish."[408] Natural laws are not negotiable, so the environmental law must comply or the efforts are in vain and the globe will continue on its trajectory toward climate catastrophe. Environmental laws in essence are domestic controls and differ by each country and even within countries (such as states in the U.S.). Whether they comply with natural law will be tested in the near future as floods, droughts and extreme weather continue to plague societies.[409]

Environmental law vis-à-vis climate change must meet a crucial test: "can it be effective in confronting the ecological challenges now coming at us with horrifying speed?" This question is "of crucial importance not only for the United States but also for other nations confronting ravenous pressure to industrialize (as well as all other nations that must endure the planetary damage wrought by overconsuming nations)."[410]

When codified into law, environmental policy can create strong conflict. As we have seen in a number of statements from denial ideologues, this conflict takes on emotional content that can defy reason. One example is the absurd claim that climate scientists are trying to dictate what everyone else does.

> ...the alarmists say that it is humans that are causing climate change. In particular, they say that it is the carbon dioxide that humans release that is making Earth warmer. They claim that earth would be a disaster if everyone doesn't give them money and do exactly as they say.[411]

"Alarmists" may be saying that CO2 makes the earth warmer, but this is based on solid climate science. The idea that science would require everyone to "*give them money and do exactly as they say*" is typical of denial ideology.

Conclusion

Success of the Paris Agreement depends on two things: continued support in the international community through follow-up negotiations, and continued support in domestic societies for low-carbon economic programs.

Denial ideology has real consequences for international negotiations. If climate scientists are seen to be dictating policy, those who resist the implications of the science will hamper politicians and negotiators. Effective responses to climate change will become difficult to reach in international fora.

More insidiously, the very existence of misinformed public opinion reduces the chances for successful outcomes. Even as the Paris Agreement is put into effect, the pressures against its successful implementation will grow. It is particularly difficult to overcome the "passive aggressive" nature of climate denial when a large segment of the public is indifferent or somewhat hostile to climate policies. This is specifically related to the issue of "lifestyles," or consumption patterns driven by cheap fossil fuel energy.

Consumption, as discussed above, drives the pace of climate change through use of fossil fuels, along with goods produced and transported with their use. This is the major factor in increasing global temperatures. Are we meeting the test? No. We are hurtling toward climate catastrophe as industries produce more and more and consumers match the high rate of production with their high rates of consumption and waste, heedless of their effects on the environment.

What is the rush? "Supreme urgency lies in the task of remaking environmental law. In view of climate crisis and a looming atmospheric 'tipping point,' society likely has only a narrow window of time remaining to steer legal institutions in a safe direction. Incremental measures will not achieve the goal; the exigencies of our time require transformative change."[412] Many scientists have concluded from their research that we have a short timeframe for preventing catastrophic climate change, and that the changes already underway will intensify even if carbon emissions were to cease. The need for "transformative change," for which so many authors have called,[413] is the driving force for many environmentalists and the source of fear among many denial ideologues. It involves some basic transformations of the world's economic and energy systems.

Will world leaders bring about this "transformative change?" Four-fifths of fossil fuels should remain in the ground if the 2-degree limit is to be realized. At the time of this writing, fossil fuel companies are spending hundreds of billions of dollars for exploration and development of new fossil fuel fields, while the reserves they already have are many times the amount that can be burned safely.

While the Paris Agreement specifies limits on emissions, societies need to go beyond the simple numbers and confront the companies and ministries that try to continue business as usual. Presidents and prime ministers must stop and reverse the growth in fossil fuels through regulations and taxes. Will world leaders put in place the enforcement mechanisms to accomplish what is needed? Otherwise we face a bleak future.

Appendix

United Nations
FCCC/CP/2015/L.9/Rev.1

Distr.: Limited   12 December 2015

Conference of the Parties Twenty-first session   Paris, 30
November to 11 December 2015

Agenda item 4(b)

Durban Platform for Enhanced Action (decision 1/CP.17)
Adoption of a protocol, another legal instrument, or an
agreed outcome with legal force under the Convention
applicable to all Parties

ADOPTION OF THE PARIS AGREEMENT

Proposal by the President

Draft decision -/CP.21

The Conference of the Parties,   Recalling decision
1/CP.17 on the establishment of the Ad Hoc Working
Group on the Durban Platform for Enhanced Action,

Also recalling Articles 2, 3 and 4 of the Convention,

Further recalling relevant decisions of the Conference of
the Parties, including decisions 1/CP.16, 2/CP.18,
1/CP.19 and 1/CP.20,

Welcoming the adoption of United Nations General
Assembly resolution A/RES/70/1, "Transforming our
world: the 2030 Agenda for Sustainable Development",
in particular its goal 13, and the adoption of the Addis
Ababa Action Agenda of the third International
Conference on Financing for Development and the
adoption of the Sendai Framework for Disaster Risk
Reduction,

Recognizing that climate change represents an urgent and potentially irreversible threat to human societies and the planet and thus requires the widest possible cooperation by all countries, and their participation in an effective and appropriate international response, with a view to accelerating the reduction of global greenhouse gas emissions,

Also recognizing that deep reductions in global emissions will be required in order to achieve the ultimate objective of the Convention and emphasizing the need for urgency in addressing climate change,

Acknowledging that climate change is a common concern of humankind, Parties should, when taking action to address climate change, respect, promote and consider their respective obligations on human rights, the right to health, the rights of indigenous peoples, local communities, migrants, children, persons with disabilities and people in vulnerable situations and the right to development, as well as gender equality, empowerment of women and intergenerational equity,

Also acknowledging the specific needs and concerns of developing country Parties arising from the impact of the implementation of response measures and, in this regard, decisions 5/CP.7, 1/CP.10, 1/CP.16 and 8/CP.17,

Emphasizing with serious concern the urgent need to address the significant gap between the aggregate effect of Parties' mitigation pledges in terms of global annual emissions of greenhouse gases by 2020 and aggregate emission pathways consistent with holding the increase in the global average temperature to well below 2 °C above pre- industrial levels and pursuing efforts to limit the temperature increase to 1.5 °C above pre- industrial levels,

Also emphasizing that enhanced pre-2020 ambition can lay a solid foundation for enhanced post-2020 ambition,

Stressing the urgency of accelerating the implementation of the Convention and its Kyoto Protocol in order to enhance pre-2020 ambition,

Recognizing the urgent need to enhance the provision of finance, technology and capacity-building support by developed country Parties, in a predictable manner, to enable enhanced pre-2020 action by developing country Parties,

Emphasizing the enduring benefits of ambitious and early action, including major reductions in the cost of future mitigation and adaptation efforts,

Acknowledging the need to promote universal access to sustainable energy in developing countries, in particular in Africa, through the enhanced deployment of renewable energy,

Agreeing to uphold and promote regional and international cooperation in order to mobilize stronger and more ambitious climate action by all Parties and non-Party stakeholders, including civil society, the private sector, financial institutions, cities and other subnational authorities, local communities and indigenous peoples,

I. ADOPTION

1. Decides to adopt the Paris Agreement under the United Nations Framework Convention on Climate Change (hereinafter referred to as "the Agreement") as contained in the annex;

2. Requests the Secretary-General of the United Nations to be the Depositary of the Agreement and to have it open for signature in New York, United States of America, from 22 April 2016 to 21 April 2017;

3. Invites the Secretary-General to convene a high-level signature ceremony for the Agreement on 22 April 2016;

4. Also invites all Parties to the Convention to sign the Agreement at the ceremony to be convened by the Secretary-General, or at their earliest opportunity, and to deposit their respective instruments of ratification, acceptance, approval or accession, where appropriate, as soon as possible;

5. Recognizes that Parties to the Convention may provisionally apply all of the provisions of the Agreement pending its entry into force, and requests Parties to provide notification of any such provisional application to the Depositary;

6. Notes that the work of the Ad Hoc Working Group on the Durban Platform for Enhanced Action, in accordance with decision 1/CP.17, paragraph 4, has been completed;

7. Decides to establish the Ad Hoc Working Group on the Paris Agreement under the same arrangement, mutatis mutandis, as those concerning the election of officers to the Bureau of the Ad Hoc Working Group on the Durban Platform for Enhanced Action;

8. Also decides that the Ad Hoc Working Group on the Paris Agreement shall prepare for the entry into force of the Agreement and for the convening of the first session of the Conference of the Parties serving as the meeting of the Parties to the Paris Agreement;

9. Further decides to oversee the implementation of the work programme resulting from the relevant requests contained in this decision;

10. Requests the Ad Hoc Working Group on the Paris Agreement to report regularly to the Conference of the Parties on the progress of its work and to complete its work by the first session of the Conference of the Parties serving as the meeting of the Parties to the Paris Agreement;

11. Decides that the Ad Hoc Working Group on the Paris

Agreement shall hold its sessions starting in 2016 in conjunction with the sessions of the Convention subsidiary bodies and shall prepare draft decisions to be recommended through the Conference of the Parties to the Conference of the Parties serving as the meeting of the Parties to the Paris Agreement for consideration and adoption at its first session;

II. INTENDED NATIONALLY DETERMINED CONTRIBUTIONS

12. Welcomes the intended nationally determined contributions that have been communicated by Parties in accordance with decision 1/CP.19, paragraph 2(b);

13. Reiterates its invitation to all Parties that have not yet done so to communicate to the secretariat their intended nationally determined contributions towards achieving the objective of the Convention as set out in its Article 2 as soon as possible and well in advance of the twenty-second session of the Conference of the Parties (November 2016) and in a manner that facilitates the clarity, transparency and understanding of the intended nationally determined contributions;

14. Requests the secretariat to continue to publish the intended nationally determined contributions communicated by Parties on the UNFCCC website;

15. Reiterates its call to developed country Parties, the operating entities of the Financial Mechanism and any other organizations in a position to do so to provide support for the preparation and communication of the intended nationally determined contributions of Parties that may need such support;

16. Takes note of the synthesis report on the aggregate effect of intended nationally determined contributions communicated by Parties by 1 October 2015, contained in document FCCC/CP/2015/7;

17. Notes with concern that the estimated aggregate greenhouse gas emission levels in 2025 and 2030 resulting from the intended nationally determined contributions do not fall within least-cost 2°C scenarios but rather lead to a projected level of 55 gigatonnes in 2030, and also notes that much greater emission reduction efforts will be required than those associated with the intended nationally determined contributions in order to hold the increase in the global average temperature to below 2°C above pre-industrial levels by reducing emissions to 40 gigatonnes or to 1.5 °C above pre-industrial levels by reducing to a level to be identified in the special report referred to in paragraph 21 below;

18. Also notes, in this context, the adaptation needs expressed by many developing country Parties in their intended nationally determined contributions;

19. Requests the secretariat to update the synthesis report referred to in paragraph 16 above so as to cover all the information in the intended nationally determined contributions communicated by Parties pursuant to decision 1/CP.20 by 4 April 2016 and to make it available by 2 May 2016;

20. Decides to convene a facilitative dialogue among Parties in 2018 to take stock of the collective efforts of Parties in relation to progress towards the long-term goal referred to in Article 4, paragraph 1, of the Agreement and to inform the preparation of nationally determined contributions pursuant to Article 4, paragraph 8, of the Agreement;

21. Invites the Intergovernmental Panel on Climate Change to provide a special report in 2018 on the impacts of global warming of 1.5 °C above pre-industrial levels and related global greenhouse gas emission pathways;

III. DECISIONS TO GIVE EFFECT TO THE AGREEMENT

22. Invites Parties to communicate their first nationally determined contribution no later than when the Party submits its respective instrument of ratification, accession, or approval of the Paris Agreement. If a Party has communicated an intended nationally determined contribution prior to joining the Agreement, that Party shall be considered to have satisfied this provision unless that Party decides otherwise;

23. Urges those Parties whose intended nationally determined contribution pursuant to decision 1/CP.20 contains a time frame up to 2025 to communicate by 2020 a new nationally determined contribution and to do so every five years thereafter pursuant to Article 4, paragraph 9, of the Agreement;

24. Requests those Parties whose intended nationally determined contribution pursuant to decision 1/CP.20 contains a time frame up to 2030 to communicate or update by 2020 these contributions and to do so every five years thereafter pursuant to Article 4, paragraph 9, of the Agreement;

25. Decides that Parties shall submit to the secretariat their nationally determined contributions referred to in Article 4 of the Agreement at least 9 to 12 months in advance of the relevant meeting of the Conference of the Parties serving as the meeting of the Parties to the Paris Agreement with a view to facilitating the clarity, transparency and understanding of these contributions, including through a synthesis report prepared by the secretariat;

26. Requests the Ad Hoc Working Group on the Paris Agreement to develop further guidance on features of the nationally determined contributions for consideration and adoption by the Conference of the Parties serving as the meeting of the Parties to the Paris Agreement at its first session;

27. Agrees that the information to be provided by Parties

communicating their nationally determined contributions, in order to facilitate clarity, transparency and understanding, may include, as appropriate, inter alia, quantifiable information on the reference point (including, as appropriate, a base year), time frames and/or periods for implementation, scope and coverage, planning processes, assumptions and methodological approaches including those for estimating and accounting for anthropogenic greenhouse gas emissions and, as appropriate, removals, and how the Party considers that its nationally determined contribution is fair and ambitious, in the light of its national circumstances, and how it contributes towards achieving the objective of the Convention as set out in its Article 2;

28. Requests the Ad Hoc Working Group on the Paris Agreement to develop further guidance for the information to be provided by Parties in order to facilitate clarity, transparency and understanding of nationally determined contributions for consideration and adoption by the Conference of the Parties serving as the meeting of the Parties to the Paris Agreement at its first session;

29. Also requests the Subsidiary Body for Implementation to develop modalities and procedures for the operation and use of the public registry referred to in Article 4, paragraph 12, of the Agreement, for consideration and adoption by the Conference of the Parties serving as the meeting of the Parties to the Paris Agreement at its first session;

30. Further requests the secretariat to make available an interim public registry in the first half of 2016 for the recording of nationally determined contributions submitted in accordance with Article 4 of the Agreement, pending the adoption by the Conference of the Parties serving as the meeting of the Parties to the Paris Agreement of the modalities and procedures referred to in paragraph 29 above;

31. Requests the Ad Hoc Working Group on the Paris

Agreement to elaborate, drawing from approaches established under the Convention and its related legal instruments as appropriate, guidance for accounting for Parties' nationally determined contributions, as referred to in Article 4, paragraph 13, of the Agreement, for consideration and adoption by the Conference of the Parties serving as the meeting of the Parties to the Paris Agreement at its first session, which ensures that:

(a) Parties account for anthropogenic emissions and removals in accordance with methodologies and common metrics assessed by the Intergovernmental Panel on Climate Change and adopted by the Conference of the Parties serving as the meeting of the Parties to the Paris Agreement;

(b) Parties ensure methodological consistency, including on baselines, between the communication and implementation of nationally determined contributions;

(c) Parties strive to include all categories of anthropogenic emissions or removals in their nationally determined contributions and, once a source, sink or activity is included, continue to include it;

(d) Parties shall provide an explanation of why any categories of anthropogenic emissions or removals are excluded;

32. Decides that Parties shall apply the guidance mentioned in paragraph 31 above to the second and subsequent nationally determined contributions and that Parties may elect to apply such guidance to their first nationally determined contribution;

33. Also decides that the Forum on the Impact of the Implementation of response measures, under the subsidiary bodies, shall continue, and shall serve the Agreement;

34. Further decides that the Subsidiary Body for

Scientific and Technological Advice and the Subsidiary Body for Implementation shall recommend, for consideration and adoption by the Conference of the Parties serving as the meeting of the Parties to the Paris Agreement at its first session, the modalities, work programme and functions of the Forum on the Impact of the Implementation of response measures to address the effects of the implementation of response measures under the Agreement by enhancing cooperation amongst Parties on understanding the impacts of mitigation actions under the Agreement and the exchange of information, experiences, and best practices amongst Parties to raise their resilience to these impacts;*

36. Invites Parties to communicate, by 2020, to the secretariat mid-century, long-term low greenhouse gas emission development strategies in accordance with Article 4, paragraph 19, of the Agreement, and requests the secretariat to publish on the UNFCCC website Parties' low greenhouse gas emission development strategies as communicated;

37. Requests the Subsidiary Body for Scientific and Technological Advice to develop and recommend the guidance referred to under Article 6, paragraph 2, of the Agreement for adoption by the Conference of the Parties serving as the meeting of the Parties to the Paris Agreement at its first session, including guidance to ensure that double counting is avoided on the basis of a corresponding adjustment by Parties for both anthropogenic emissions by sources and removals by sinks covered by their nationally determined contributions under the Agreement;

38. Recommends that the Conference of the Parties serving as the meeting of the Parties to the Paris Agreement adopt rules, modalities and procedures for the mechanism established by Article 6, paragraph 4, of the Agreement on the basis of:

. (a) Voluntary participation authorized by each Party

involved;

. (b) Real, measurable, and long-term benefits related to the mitigation of climate

change;

(c) Specific scopes of activities;

(d) Reductions in emissions that are additional to any that would otherwise occur;

(e) Verification and certification of emission reductions resulting from mitigation activities by designated operational entities;

(f) Experience gained with and lessons learned from existing mechanisms and approaches adopted under the Convention and its related legal instruments;

39. Requests the Subsidiary Body for Scientific and Technological Advice to develop and recommend rules, modalities and procedures for the mechanism referred to in paragraph 38 above for consideration and adoption by the Conference of the Parties serving as the meeting of the Parties to the Paris Agreement at its first session;

40. Also requests the Subsidiary Body for Scientific and Technological Advice to undertake a work programme under the framework for non-market approaches to sustainable development referred to in Article 6, paragraph 8, of the Agreement, with the objective of considering how to enhance linkages and create synergy between, inter alia, mitigation, adaptation, finance, technology transfer and capacity-building, and how to facilitate the implementation and coordination of non-market approaches;

41. Further requests the Subsidiary Body for Scientific and Technological Advice to recommend a draft decision on the work programme referred to in paragraph 40

above, taking into account the views of Parties, for consideration and adoption by the Conference of the Parties serving as the meeting of the Parties to the Paris Agreement at its first session;

ADAPTATION

42. Requests the Adaptation Committee and the Least Developed Countries Expert Group to jointly develop modalities to recognize the adaptation efforts of developing country Parties, as referred to in Article 7, paragraph 3, of the Agreement, and make recommendations for consideration and adoption by the Conference of the Parties serving as the meeting of the Parties to the Paris Agreement at its first session;

43. Also requests the Adaptation Committee, taking into account its mandate and its second three-year workplan, and with a view to preparing recommendations for consideration and adoption by the Conference of the Parties serving as the meeting of the Parties to the Paris Agreement at its first session:

(a) To review, in 2017, the work of adaptation-related institutional arrangements under the Convention, with a view to identifying ways to enhance the coherence of their work, as appropriate, in order to respond adequately to the needs of Parties;

(b) To consider methodologies for assessing adaptation needs with a view to assisting developing countries, without placing an undue burden on them;

44. Invites all relevant United Nations agencies and international, regional and national financial institutions to provide information to Parties through the secretariat on how their development assistance and climate finance programmes incorporate climate-proofing and climate resilience measures;

45. Requests Parties to strengthen regional cooperation on

adaptation where appropriate and, where necessary, establish regional centres and networks, in particular in developing countries, taking into account decision 1/CP.16, paragraph 13;

46. Also requests the Adaptation Committee and the Least Developed Countries Expert Group, in collaboration with the Standing Committee on Finance and other relevant institutions, to develop methodologies, and make recommendations for consideration and adoption by the Conference of the Parties serving as the meeting of the Parties to the Paris Agreement at its first session on:

(a) Taking the necessary steps to facilitate the mobilization of support for adaptation in developing countries in the context of the limit to global average temperature increase referred to in Article 2 of the Agreement;

(b) Reviewing the adequacy and effectiveness of adaptation and support referred to in Article 7, paragraph 14(c), of the Agreement;

47. Further requests the Green Climate Fund to expedite support for the least developed countries and other developing country Parties for the formulation of national adaptation plans, consistent with decisions 1/CP.16 and 5/CP.17, and for the subsequent implementation of policies, projects and programmes identified by them;

LOSS AND DAMAGE

48. Decides on the continuation of the Warsaw International Mechanism for Loss and

Damage associated with Climate Change Impacts, following the review in 2016;

49. Requests the Executive Committee of the Warsaw International Mechanism to establish a clearinghouse for

risk transfer that serves as a repository for information on insurance and risk transfer, in order to facilitate the efforts of Parties to develop and implement comprehensive risk management strategies;

50. Also requests the Executive Committee of the Warsaw International Mechanism to establish, according to its procedures and mandate, a task force to complement, draw upon the work of and involve, as appropriate, existing bodies and expert groups under the Convention including the Adaptation Committee and the Least Developed Countries Expert Group, as well as relevant organizations and expert bodies outside the Convention, to develop recommendations for integrated approaches to avert, minimize and address displacement related to the adverse impacts of climate change;

51. Further requests the Executive Committee of the Warsaw International Mechanism to initiate its work, at its next meeting, to operationalize the provisions referred to in paragraphs 49 and 50 above, and to report on progress thereon in its annual report;

52. Agrees that Article 8 of the Agreement does not involve or provide a basis for any liability or compensation;

FINANCE

53. Decides that, in the implementation of the Agreement, financial resources provided to developing countries should enhance the implementation of their policies, strategies, regulations and action plans and their climate change actions with respect to both mitigation and adaptation to contribute to the achievement of the purpose of the Agreement as defined in Article 2;

54. Also decides that, in accordance with Article 9, paragraph 3, of the Agreement, developed countries intend to continue their existing collective mobilization goal through 2025 in the context of meaningful mitigation

actions and transparency on implementation; prior to 2025 the Conference of the Parties serving as the meeting of the Parties to the Paris Agreement shall set a new collective quantified goal from a floor of USD 100 billion per year, taking into account the needs and priorities of developing countries;

55. Recognizes the importance of adequate and predictable financial resources, including for results-based payments, as appropriate, for the implementation of policy approaches and positive incentives for reducing emissions from deforestation and forest degradation, and the role of conservation, sustainable management of forests and enhancement of forest carbon stocks; as well as alternative policy approaches, such as joint mitigation and adaptation approaches for the integral and sustainable management of forests; while reaffirming the importance of non-carbon benefits associated with such approaches; encouraging the coordination of support from, inter alia, public and private, bilateral and multilateral sources, such as the Green Climate Fund, and alternative sources in accordance with relevant decisions by the Conference of the Parties;

56. Decides to initiate, at its twenty-second session, a process to identify the information to be provided by Parties, in accordance with Article 9, paragraph 5, of the Agreement with the view to providing a recommendation for consideration and adoption by the Conference of the Parties serving as the meeting of the Parties to the Paris Agreement at its first session;

57. Also decides to ensure that the provision of information in accordance with Article 9, paragraph 7 of the Agreement shall be undertaken in accordance with modalities, procedures and guidelines referred to in paragraph 96 below;

58. Requests Subsidiary Body for Scientific and Technological Advice to develop modalities for the accounting of financial resources provided and mobilized

through public interventions in accordance with Article 9, paragraph 7, of the Agreement for consideration by the Conference of the Parties at its twenty-fourth session (November 2018), with the view to making a recommendation for consideration and adoption by the Conference of the Parties serving as the meeting of the Parties to the Paris Agreement at its first session;

59. Decides that the Green Climate Fund and the Global Environment Facility, the entities entrusted with the operation of the Financial Mechanism of the Convention, as well as the Least Developed Countries Fund and the Special Climate Change Fund, administered by the Global Environment Facility, shall serve the Agreement;

60. Recognizes that the Adaptation Fund may serve the Agreement, subject to relevant decisions by the Conference of the Parties serving as the meeting of the Parties to the Kyoto Protocol and the Conference of the Parties serving as the meeting of the Parties to the Paris Agreement;

61. Invites the Conference of the Parties serving as the meeting of the Parties to the Kyoto Protocol to consider the issue referred to in paragraph 60 above and make a recommendation to the Conference of the Parties serving as the meeting of the Parties to the Paris Agreement at its first session;

62. Recommends that the Conference of the Parties serving as the meeting of the Parties to the Paris Agreement shall provide guidance to the entities entrusted with the operation of the Financial Mechanism of the Convention on the policies, programme priorities and eligibility criteria related to the Agreement for transmission by the Conference of the Parties;

63. Decides that the guidance to the entities entrusted with the operations of the Financial Mechanism of the Convention in relevant decisions of the Conference of the Parties, including those agreed before adoption of the

Agreement, shall apply mutatis mutandis;

64. Also decides that the Standing Committee on Finance shall serve the Agreement in line with its functions and responsibilities established under the Conference of the Parties;

65. Urges the institutions serving the Agreement to enhance the coordination and delivery of resources to support country-driven strategies through simplified and efficient application and approval procedures, and through continued readiness support to developing country Parties, including the least developed countries and small island developing States, as appropriate;

TECHNOLOGY DEVELOPMENT AND TRANSFER

66. Takes note of the interim report of the Technology Executive Committee on guidance on enhanced implementation of the results of technology needs assessments as referred to in document FCCC/SB/2015/INF.3;

67. Decides to strengthen the Technology Mechanism and requests the Technology Executive Committee and the Climate Technology Centre and Network, in supporting the implementation of the Agreement, to undertake further work relating to, inter alia:

(a) Technology research, development and demonstration;

(b) The development and enhancement of endogenous capacities and technologies;

68. Requests the Subsidiary Body for Scientific and Technological Advice to initiate, at its forty-fourth session (May 2016), the elaboration of the technology framework established under Article 10, paragraph 4, of the Agreement and to report on its findings to the Conference of the Parties, with a view to the Conference of the Parties making a recommendation on the

framework to the Conference of the Parties serving as the meeting of the Parties to the Paris Agreement for consideration and adoption at its first session, taking into consideration that the framework should facilitate, inter alia:

(a) The undertaking and updating of technology needs assessments, as well as the enhanced implementation of their results, particularly technology action plans and project ideas, through the preparation of bankable projects;

(b) The provision of enhanced financial and technical support for the implementation of the results of the technology needs assessments;

(c) The assessment of technologies that are ready for transfer;   (d) The enhancement of enabling environments for and the addressing of barriers

to the development and transfer of socially and environmentally sound technologies;

69. Decides that the Technology Executive Committee and the Climate Technology Centre and Network shall report to the Conference of the Parties serving as the meeting of the Parties to the Paris Agreement, through the subsidiary bodies, on their activities to support the implementation of the Agreement;

70. Also decides to undertake a periodic assessment of the effectiveness of and the adequacy of the support provided to the Technology Mechanism in supporting the implementation of the Agreement on matters relating to technology development and transfer;

71. Requests the Subsidiary Body for Implementation to initiate, at its forty-fourth session , the elaboration of the scope of and modalities for the periodic assessment referred to in paragraph 70 above, taking into account the review of the Climate Technology Centre and Network as

referred to in decision 2/CP.17, annex VII, paragraph 20 and the modalities for the global stocktake referred to in Article 14 of the Agreement, for consideration and adoption by the Conference of the Parties at its twenty-fifth session (November 2019);

CAPACITY-BUILDING

72. Decides to establish the Paris Committee on Capacity-building whose aim will be to address gaps and needs, both current and emerging, in implementing capacity-building in developing country Parties and further enhancing capacity-building efforts, including with regard to coherence and coordination in capacity-building activities under the Convention;

73. Also decides that the Paris Committee on Capacity-building will manage and oversee the work plan mentioned in paragraph 74 below;

74. Further decides to launch a work plan for the period 2016–2020 with the following activities:

(a) Assessing how to increase synergies through cooperation and avoid duplication among existing bodies established under the Convention that implement capacity-building activities, including through collaborating with institutions under and outside the Convention;

(b) Identifying capacity gaps and needs and recommending ways to address them;

(c) Promoting the development and dissemination of tools and methodologies for the implementation of capacity-building;

. (d) Fostering global, regional, national and subnational cooperation;

. (e) Identifying and collecting good practices,

challenges, experiences, and

lessons learned from work on capacity-building by bodies established under the Convention;

(f) Exploring how developing country Parties can take ownership of building and maintaining capacity over time and space;

(g) Identifying opportunities to strengthen capacity at the national, regional, and subnational level;

(h) Fostering dialogue, coordination, collaboration and coherence among relevant processes and initiatives under the Convention, including through exchanging information on capacity-building activities and strategies of bodies established under the Convention;

(i) Providing guidance to the secretariat on the maintenance and further development of the web-based capacity-building portal;

75. Decides that the Paris Committee on Capacity-building will annually focus on an area or theme related to enhanced technical exchange on capacity-building, with the purpose of maintaining up-to-date knowledge on the successes and challenges in building capacity effectively in a particular area;

76. Requests the Subsidiary Body for Implementation to organize annual in-session meetings of the Paris Committee on Capacity-building;

77. Also requests the Subsidiary Body for Implementation to develop the terms of reference for the Paris Committee on Capacity-building, in the context of the third comprehensive review of the implementation of the capacity-building framework, also taking into account paragraphs 75, 76, 77 and 78 above and paragraphs 82 and 83 below, with a view to recommending a draft decision on this matter for consideration and adoption by

the Conference of the Parties at its twenty-second session;

78. Invites Parties to submit their views on the membership of the Paris Committee on Capacity-building by 9 March 2016;

79. Requests the secretariat to compile the submissions referred to in paragraph 78 above into a miscellaneous document for consideration by the Subsidiary Body for Implementation at its forty-fourth session;

80. Decides that the inputs to the Paris Committee on Capacity-building will include, inter alia, submissions, the outcome of the third comprehensive review of the implementation of the capacity-building framework, the secretariat's annual synthesis report on the implementation of the framework for capacity-building in developing countries, the secretariat's compilation and synthesis report on capacity-building work of bodies established under the Convention and its Kyoto Protocol, and reports on the Durban Forum and the capacity-building portal;

81. Requests the Paris Committee on Capacity-building to prepare annual technical progress reports on its work, and to make these reports available at the sessions of the Subsidiary Body for Implementation coinciding with the sessions of the Conference of the Parties;

82. Also requests the Conference of the Parties at its twenty-fifth session (November 2019), to review the progress, need for extension, the effectiveness and enhancement of the Paris Committee on Capacity-building and to take any action it considers appropriate, with a view to making recommendations to the Conference of the Parties serving as the meeting of the Parties to the Paris Agreement at its first session on enhancing institutional arrangements for capacity-building consistent with Article 11, paragraph 5, of the Agreement;

83. Calls upon all Parties to ensure that education, training and public awareness, as reflected in Article 6 of the Convention and in Article 12 of the Agreement are adequately considered in their contribution to capacity-building;

84. Invites the Conference of the Parties serving as the meeting of the Parties to the Paris Agreement at its first session to explore ways of enhancing the implementation of training, public awareness, public participation and public access to information so as to enhance actions under the Agreement;

TRANSPARENCY OF ACTION AND SUPPORT

85. Decides to establish a Capacity-building Initiative for Transparency in order to build institutional and technical capacity, both pre- and post-2020. This initiative will support developing country Parties, upon request, in meeting enhanced transparency requirements as defined in Article 13 of the Agreement in a timely manner;

86. Also decides that the Capacity-building Initiative for Transparency will aim: (a) To strengthen national institutions for transparency-related activities in line with national priorities;

(b) To provide relevant tools, training and assistance for meeting the provisions stipulated in Article 13 of the Agreement;

(c) To assist in the improvement of transparency over time;

87. Urges and requests the Global Environment Facility to make arrangements to support the establishment and operation of the Capacity-building Initiative for Transparency as a priority reporting-related need, including through voluntary contributions to support developing countries in the sixth replenishment of the Global Environment Facility and future replenishment

cycles, to complement existing support under the Global Environment Facility;

88. Decides to assess the implementation of the Capacity-building Initiative for Transparency in the context of the seventh review of the financial mechanism;

89. Requests that the Global Environment Facility, as an operating entity of the financial mechanism include in its annual report to the Conference of the Parties the progress of work in the design, development and implementation of the Capacity-building Initiative for Transparency referred to in paragraph 85 above starting in 2016;

90. Decides that, in accordance with Article 13, paragraph 2, of the Agreement, developing countries shall be provided flexibility in the implementation of the provisions of that Article, including in the scope, frequency and level of detail of reporting, and in the scope of review, and that the scope of review could provide for in-country reviews to be optional, while such flexibilities shall be reflected in the development of modalities, procedures and guidelines referred to in paragraph 92 below;

91. Also decides that all Parties, except for the least developed country Parties and small island developing States, shall submit the information referred to in Article 13, paragraphs 7, 8, 9 and 10, as appropriate, no less frequently than on a biennial basis, and that the least developed country Parties and small island developing States may submit this information at their discretion;

92. Requests the Ad Hoc Working Group on the Paris Agreement to develop recommendations for modalities, procedures and guidelines in accordance with Article 13, paragraph 13, of the Agreement, and to define the year of their first and subsequent review and update, as appropriate, at regular intervals, for consideration by the Conference of the Parties, at its twenty-fourth session, with a view to forwarding them to the Conference of the

Parties serving as the meeting of the Parties to the Paris Agreement for adoption at its first session;

93. Also requests the Ad Hoc Working Group on the Paris Agreement in developing the recommendations for the modalities, procedures and guidelines referred to in paragraph 92 above to take into account, inter alia:

(a) The importance of facilitating improved reporting and transparency over time;

(b) The need to provide flexibility to those developing country Parties that need it in the light of their capacities;

(c) The need to promote transparency, accuracy, completeness, consistency, and comparability;

(d) The need to avoid duplication as well as undue burden on Parties and the secretariat;

(e) The need to ensure that Parties maintain at least the frequency and quality of reporting in accordance with their respective obligations under the Convention;

. (f) The need to ensure that double counting is avoided;

. (g) The need to ensure environmental integrity;

94. Further requests the Ad Hoc Working Group on the Paris Agreement, when developing the modalities, procedures and guidelines referred to in paragraph 92 above, to draw on the experiences from and take into account other on-going relevant processes under the Convention;

95. Requests the Ad Hoc Working Group on the Paris Agreement, when developing modalities, procedures and guidelines referred to in paragraph 92 above, to consider, inter alia:

(a) The types of flexibility available to those developing

countries that need it on the basis of their capacities;

(b) The consistency between the methodology communicated in the nationally determined contribution and the methodology for reporting on progress made towards achieving individual Parties' respective nationally determined contribution;

(c) That Parties report information on adaptation action and planning including, if appropriate, their national adaptation plans, with a view to collectively exchanging information and sharing lessons learned;

(d) Support provided, enhancing delivery of support for both adaptation and mitigation through, inter alia, the common tabular formats for reporting support, and taking into account issues considered by the Subsidiary Body for Scientific and Technological Advice on methodologies for reporting on financial information, and enhancing the reporting by developing countries on support received, including the use, impact and estimated results thereof;

(e) Information in the biennial assessments and other reports of the Standing Committee on Finance and other relevant bodies under the Convention;

(f) Information on the social and economic impact of response measures;

96. Also requests the Ad Hoc Working Group on the Paris Agreement, when developing recommendations for modalities, procedures and guidelines referred to in paragraph 92 above, to enhance the transparency of support provided in accordance with Article 9 of the Agreement;

97. Further requests the Ad Hoc Working Group on the Paris Agreement to report on the progress of work on the modalities, procedures and guidelines referred to in paragraph 92 above to future sessions of the Conference of the Parties, and that this work be concluded no later

than 2018;

98. Decides that the modalities, procedures and guidelines developed under paragraph 92 above, shall be applied upon the entry into force of the Paris Agreement;

99. Also decides that the modalities, procedures and guidelines of this transparency framework shall build upon and eventually supersede the measurement, reporting and verification system established by decision 1/CP.16, paragraphs 40 to 47 and 60 to 64, and decision 2/CP.17, paragraphs 12 to 62, immediately following the submission of the final biennial reports and biennial update reports;

GLOBAL STOCKTAKE

100. Requests the Ad Hoc Working Group on the Paris Agreement to identify the sources of input for the global stocktake referred to in Article 14 of the Agreement and to report to the Conference of the Parties, with a view to the Conference of the Parties making a recommendation to the Conference of the Parties serving as the meeting of the Parties to the Paris Agreement for consideration and adoption at its first session, including, but not limited to:

(a) Information on:

(i) The overall effect of the nationally determined contributions communicated by Parties;

(ii) The state of adaptation efforts, support, experiences and priorities from the communications referred to in Article 7, paragraphs 10 and 11, of the Agreement, and reports referred to in Article 13, paragraph 7, of the Agreement;

(iii) The mobilization and provision of support;

. (b) The latest reports of the Intergovernmental Panel on Climate Change;

. (c) Reports of the subsidiary bodies;

101. Also requests the Subsidiary Body for Scientific and Technological Advice to provide advice on how the assessments of the Intergovernmental Panel on Climate Change can inform the global stocktake of the implementation of the Agreement pursuant to its Article 14 of the Agreement and to report on this matter to the Ad Hoc Working Group on the Paris Agreement at its second session;

102. Further requests the Ad Hoc Working Group on the Paris Agreement to develop modalities for the global stocktake referred to in Article 14 of the Agreement and to report to the Conference of the Parties, with a view to making a recommendation to the Conference of the Parties serving as the meeting of the Parties to the Paris Agreement for consideration and adoption at its first session;

FACILITATING IMPLEMENTATION AND COMPLIANCE

103. Decides that the committee referred to in Article 15, paragraph 2, of the Agreement shall consist of 12 members with recognized competence in relevant scientific, technical, socio-economic or legal fields, to be elected by the Conference of the Parties serving as the meeting of the Parties to the Paris Agreement on the basis of equitable geographical representation, with two members each from the five regional groups of the United Nations and one member each from the small island developing States and the least developed countries, while taking into account the goal of gender balance;

104. Requests the Ad Hoc Working Group on the Paris Agreement to develop the modalities and procedures for the effective operation of the committee referred to in Article 15, paragraph 2, of the Agreement, with a view to the Ad Hoc Working Group on the Paris

Agreement completing its work on such modalities and procedures for consideration and adoption by the Conference of the Parties serving as the meeting of the Parties to the Paris Agreement at its first session;

FINAL CLAUSES

105. Also requests the secretariat, solely for the purposes of Article 21 of the Agreement, to make available on its website on the date of adoption of the Agreement as well as in the report of the Conference of the Parties at its twenty-first session, information on the most up-to-date total and per cent of greenhouse gas emissions communicated by Parties to the Convention in their national communications, greenhouse gas inventory reports, biennial reports or biennial update reports;

IV. ENHANCED ACTION PRIOR TO 2020

106. Resolves to ensure the highest possible mitigation efforts in the pre-2020 period, including by:

(a) Urging all Parties to the Kyoto Protocol that have not already done so to ratify and implement the Doha Amendment to the Kyoto Protocol;

(b) Urging all Parties that have not already done so to make and implement a mitigation pledge under the Cancun Agreements;

(c) Reiterating its resolve, as set out in decision 1/CP.19, paragraphs 3 and 4, to accelerate the full implementation of the decisions constituting the agreed outcome pursuant to decision 1/CP.13 and enhance ambition in the pre-2020 period in order to ensure the highest possible mitigation efforts under the Convention by all Parties;

(d) Inviting developing country Parties that have not submitted their first biennial update reports to do so as soon as possible;

(e) Urging all Parties to participate in the existing measurement, reporting and verification processes under the Cancun Agreements, in a timely manner, with a view to demonstrating progress made in the implementation of their mitigation pledges;

107. Encourages Parties to promote the voluntary cancellation by Party and non-Party stakeholders, without double counting of units issued under the Kyoto Protocol, including certified emission reductions that are valid for the second commitment period;

108. Urges host and purchasing Parties to report transparently on internationally transferred mitigation outcomes, including outcomes used to meet international pledges, and emission units issued under the Kyoto Protocol with a view to promoting environmental integrity and avoiding double counting;

109. Recognizes the social, economic and environmental value of voluntary mitigation actions and their co-benefits for adaptation, health and sustainable development;

110. Resolves to strengthen, in the period 2016–2020, the existing technical examination process on mitigation as defined in decision 1/CP.19, paragraph 5(a), and decision 1/CP.20, paragraph 19, taking into account the latest scientific knowledge, including by:

(a) Encouraging Parties, Convention bodies and international organizations to engage in this process, including, as appropriate, in cooperation with relevant non-Party stakeholders, to share their experiences and suggestions, including from regional events, and to cooperate in facilitating the implementation of policies, practices and actions identified during this process in accordance with national sustainable development priorities;

(b) Striving to improve, in consultation with Parties, access to and participation in this process by developing country Party and non-Party experts;

(c) Requesting the Technology Executive Committee and the Climate Technology Centre and Network in accordance with their respective mandates:

(i) To engage in the technical expert meetings and enhance their efforts to facilitate and support Parties in scaling up the implementation of policies, practices and actions identified during this process;

(ii) To provide regular updates during the technical expert meetings on the progress made in facilitating the implementation of policies, practices and actions previously identified during this process;

(iii) To include information on their activities under this process in their joint annual report to the Conference of the Parties;

(d) Encouraging Parties to make effective use of the Climate Technology Centre and Network to obtain assistance to develop economically, environmentally and socially viable project proposals in the high mitigation potential areas identified in this process;

111. Encourages the operating entities of the Financial Mechanism of the Convention to engage in the technical expert meetings and to inform participants of their contribution to facilitating progress in the implementation of policies, practices and actions identified during the technical examination process;

112. Requests the secretariat to organize the process referred to in paragraph 110 above and disseminate its results, including by:

(a) Organizing, in consultation with the Technology Executive Committee and relevant expert organizations, regular technical expert meetings focusing on specific policies, practices and actions representing best practices and with the potential to be scalable and replicable;

(b) Updating, on an annual basis, following the meetings referred to in paragraph 112(a) above and in time to serve as input to the summary for policymakers referred to in paragraph 112(c) below, a technical paper on the mitigation benefits and co-benefits of policies, practices and actions for enhancing mitigation ambition, as well as on options for supporting their implementation, information on which should be made available in a user-friendly online format;

(c) Preparing, in consultation with the champions referred to in paragraph 122 below, a summary for policymakers, with information on specific policies, practices and actions representing best practices and with the potential to be scalable and replicable, and on options to support their implementation, as well as on relevant collaborative initiatives, and publishing the summary at least two months in advance of each session of the Conference of the Parties as input for the high-level event referred to in paragraph 121 below;

113. Decides that the process referred to in paragraph 110 above should be organized jointly by the Subsidiary Body for Implementation and the Subsidiary Body for Scientific and Technological Advice and should take place on an ongoing basis until 2020;

114. Also decides to conduct in 2017 an assessment of the process referred to in paragraph 110 above so as to improve its effectiveness;

115. Resolves to enhance the provision of urgent and adequate finance, technology and capacity-building support by developed country Parties in order to enhance the level of ambition of pre-2020 action by Parties, and in this regard strongly urges developed country Parties to scale up their level of financial support, with a concrete roadmap to achieve the

goal of jointly providing USD 100 billion annually by 2020 for mitigation and adaptation while significantly increasing adaptation finance from current levels and to further provide appropriate technology and capacity-building support;

116. Decides to conduct a facilitative dialogue in conjunction with the twenty-second session of the Conference of the Parties to assess the progress in implementing decision 1/CP.19, paragraphs 3 and 4, and identify relevant opportunities to enhance the provision of financial resources, including for technology development and transfer and capacity- building support, with a view to identifying ways to enhance the ambition of mitigation efforts by all Parties, including identifying relevant opportunities to enhance the provision and mobilization of support and enabling environments;

117. Acknowledges with appreciation the results of the Lima-Paris Action Agenda, which build on the climate summit convened on 23 September 2014 by the Secretary-General of the United Nations;

118. Welcomes the efforts of non-Party stakeholders to scale up their climate actions, and encourages the registration of those actions in the Non-State Actor Zone for Climate Action platform;[3]

119. Encourages Parties to work closely with non-Party stakeholders to catalyse efforts to strengthen mitigation and adaptation action;

120. Also encourages non-Party stakeholders to increase their engagement in the processes referred to in paragraph 110 above and paragraph 125 below;

121. Agrees to convene, pursuant to decision 1/CP.20, paragraph 21, building on the Lima-Paris Action Agenda and in conjunction with each session of the Conference of the Parties during the period 2016–2020, a high-level event that:

(a) Further strengthens high-level engagement on the implementation of policy options and actions arising from the processes referred to in paragraph 110 above and paragraph 125 below, drawing on the summary for policymakers referred to in paragraph 112(c) above;

(b) Provides an opportunity for announcing new or strengthened voluntary efforts, initiatives and coalitions, including the implementation of policies, practices and actions arising from the processes referred to in paragraph 110 above and paragraph 125 below and presented in the summary for policymakers referred to in paragraph 112(c) above;

(c) Takes stock of related progress and recognizes new or strengthened voluntary efforts, initiatives and coalitions;

(d) Provides meaningful and regular opportunities for the effective high-level engagement of dignitaries of Parties, international organizations, international cooperative initiatives and non-Party stakeholders;

122. Decides that two high-level champions shall be appointed to act on behalf of the President of the Conference of the Parties to facilitate through strengthened high-level engagement in the period 2016–2020 the successful execution of existing efforts and the scaling-up and introduction of new or strengthened voluntary efforts, initiatives and coalitions, including by:

3 <http://climateaction.unfccc.int/>.

(a) Working with the Executive Secretary and the current and incoming Presidents of the Conference of the Parties to coordinate the annual high-level event referred to in paragraph 121 above;

(b) Engaging with interested Parties and non-Party stakeholders, including to further the voluntary initiatives of the Lima-Paris Action Agenda;

(c) Providing guidance to the secretariat on the organization of technical expert meetings referred to in paragraph 112(a) above and paragraph 130(a) below;

123. Also decides that the high-level champions referred to in paragraph 122 above should normally serve for a term of two years, with their terms overlapping for a full year to ensure continuity, such that:

(a) The President of the Conference of the Parties of the twenty-first session should appoint one champion, who should serve for one year from the date of the appointment until the last day of the Conference of the Parties at its twenty-second session;

(b) The President of the Conference of the Parties of the twenty-second session should appoint one champion who should serve for two years from the date of the appointment until the last day of the Conference of the Parties at its twenty-third session (November 2017);

(c) Thereafter, each subsequent President of the Conference of the Parties should appoint one champion who should serve for two years and succeed the previously appointed champion whose term has ended;

124. Invites all interested Parties and relevant organizations to provide support for the work of the champions referred to in paragraph 122 above;

125. Decides to launch, in the period 2016–2020, a technical examination process on adaptation;

126. Also decides that the technical examination process on adaptation referred to in paragraph 125 above will endeavour to identify concrete opportunities for strengthening resilience, reducing vulnerabilities and increasing the understanding and implementation of adaptation actions;

127. Further decides that the technical examination

process referred to in paragraph 125 above should be organized jointly by the Subsidiary Body for Implementation and the Subsidiary Body for Scientific and Technological Advice, and conducted by the Adaptation Committee;

128. Decides that the process referred to in paragraph 125 above will be pursued by:

. (a) Facilitating the sharing of good practices, experiences and lessons learned;

. (b) Identifying actions that could significantly enhance the implementation of

adaptation actions, including actions that could enhance economic diversification and have mitigation co-benefits;

(c) Promoting cooperative action on adaptation;

(d) Identifying opportunities to strengthen enabling environments and enhance the provision of support for adaptation in the context of specific policies, practices and actions;

129. Also decides that the technical examination process on adaptation referred to in paragraph 125 above will take into account the process, modalities, outputs, outcomes and lessons learned from the technical examination process on mitigation referred to in paragraph 110 above;

130. Requests the secretariat to support the technical examination process referred to in paragraph 125 above by:

(a) Organizing regular technical expert meetings focusing on specific policies, strategies and actions;

(b) Preparing annually, on the basis of the meetings referred to in paragraph 130(a) above and in time to serve as an input to the summary for policymakers referred to in paragraph 112(c) above, a technical paper on opportunities to enhance adaptation action, as well as options to support their implementation, information on which should be made available in a user-friendly online format;

131. Decides that in conducting the process referred to in paragraph 125 above, the Adaptation Committee will engage with and explore ways to take into account, synergize with and build on the existing arrangements for adaptation-related work programmes, bodies and institutions under the Convention so as to ensure coherence and maximum value;

132. Also decides to conduct, in conjunction with the assessment referred to in paragraph 120 above, an assessment of the process referred to in paragraph 125 above, so as to improve its effectiveness;

133. Invites Parties and observer organizations to submit information on the opportunities referred to in paragraph 126 above by 3 February 2016;

V. NON-PARTY STAKEHOLDERS

134. Welcomes the efforts of all non-Party stakeholders to address and respond to climate change, including those of civil society, the private sector, financial institutions, cities and other subnational authorities;

135. Invites the non-Party stakeholders referred to in paragraph 134 above to scale up their efforts and support actions to reduce emissions and/or to build resilience and decrease vulnerability to the adverse effects of climate change and demonstrate these efforts via the Non-State Actor Zone for Climate Action platform[4] referred to in paragraph 118 above;

136. Recognizes the need to strengthen knowledge, technologies, practices and efforts of local communities and indigenous peoples related to addressing and responding to climate change, and establishes a platform

for the exchange of experiences and sharing of best practices on mitigation and adaptation in a holistic and integrated manner;

137. Also recognizes the important role of providing incentives for emission reduction activities, including tools such as domestic policies and carbon pricing;

VI. ADMINISTRATIVE AND BUDGETARY MATTERS

138. Takes note of the estimated budgetary implications of the activities to be undertaken by the secretariat referred to in this decision and requests that the actions of the secretariat called for in this decision be undertaken subject to the availability of financial resources;

139. Emphasizes the urgency of making additional resources available for the implementation of the relevant actions, including actions referred to in this decision, and the implementation of the work programme referred to in paragraph 9 above;

[4] <http://climateaction.unfccc.int/>.

140. Urges Parties to make voluntary contributions for the timely implementation of this decision.

Being Parties to the United Nations Framework Convention on Climate Change, hereinafter referred to as "the Convention",

Pursuant to the Durban Platform for Enhanced Action established by decision 1/CP.17 of the Conference of the Parties to the Convention at its seventeenth session,

In pursuit of the objective of the Convention, and being guided by its principles, including the principle of equity and common but differentiated responsibilities and respective capabilities, in the light of different national circumstances,

Recognizing the need for an effective and progressive response to the urgent threat of climate change on the basis of the best available scientific knowledge,

Also recognizing the specific needs and special circumstances of developing country Parties, especially those that are particularly vulnerable to the adverse effects of climate change, as provided for in the Convention,

Taking full account of the specific needs and special situations of the least developed countries with regard to funding and transfer of technology,

Recognizing that Parties may be affected not only by climate change, but also by the impacts of the measures taken in response to it,

Emphasizing the intrinsic relationship that climate change actions, responses and impacts have with equitable access to sustainable development and eradication of poverty,

Recognizing the fundamental priority of safeguarding food security and ending hunger, and the particular vulnerabilities of food production systems to the adverse impacts of climate change,

Taking into account the imperatives of a just transition of the workforce and the creation of decent work and quality jobs in accordance with nationally defined development priorities,

Acknowledging that climate change is a common concern of humankind, Parties should, when taking action to address climate change, respect, promote and consider their respective obligations on human rights, the right to health, the rights of indigenous peoples, local communities, migrants, children, persons with disabilities and people in vulnerable situations and the right to development, as well as gender equality, empowerment of women and intergenerational equity,

Recognizing the importance of the conservation and enhancement, as appropriate, of sinks and reservoirs of the greenhouse gases referred to in the Convention,

Noting the importance of ensuring the integrity of all ecosystems, including oceans, and the protection of biodiversity, recognized by some cultures as Mother Earth, and noting the importance for some of the concept of "climate justice", when taking action to address climate change,

Affirming the importance of education, training, public awareness, public participation, public access to information and cooperation at all levels on the matters addressed in this Agreement,

Recognizing the importance of the engagements of all levels of government and various actors, in accordance with respective national legislations of Parties, in addressing climate change,

Also recognizing that sustainable lifestyles and sustainable patterns of consumption and production, with developed country Parties taking the lead, play an important role in addressing climate change,

The Parties to this Agreement, Have agreed as follows:

PARIS AGREEMENT

Article 1

For the purpose of this Agreement, the definitions contained in Article 1 of the Convention shall apply. In addition:

1. "Convention" means the United Nations Framework Convention on Climate Change, adopted in New York on 9 May 1992.

2. "Conference of the Parties" means the Conference of the Parties to the Convention.

3. "Party" means a Party to this Agreement.

Article 2

1. This Agreement, in enhancing the implementation of the Convention, including its objective, aims to strengthen the global response to the threat of climate change, in the context of sustainable development and efforts to eradicate poverty, including by:

    (a) Holding the increase in the global average temperature to well below 2 °C above pre-industrial levels and to pursue efforts to limit the temperature increase to 1.5 °C above pre-industrial levels, recognizing that this would significantly reduce the risks and impacts of climate change;

(b) Increasing the ability to adapt to the adverse impacts of climate change and foster climate resilience and low greenhouse gas emissions development, in a manner that does not threaten food production;

(c) Making finance flows consistent with a pathway towards low greenhouse gas emissions and climate- resilient development.

2. This Agreement will be implemented to reflect equity and the principle of common but differentiated responsibilities and respective capabilities, in the light of different national circumstances.

Article 3

As nationally determined contributions to the global response to climate change, all Parties are to undertake and communicate ambitious efforts as defined in Articles 4, 7, 9, 10, 11 and 13 with the view to achieving the purpose of this Agreement as set out in Article 2. The efforts of all Parties will represent a progression over time, while recognizing the need to support developing country Parties for the effective implementation of this Agreement.

Article 4

1. In order to achieve the long-term temperature goal set out in Article 2, Parties aim to reach global peaking of greenhouse gas emissions as soon as possible, recognizing that peaking will take longer for developing country Parties, and to undertake rapid reductions thereafter in accordance with best available science, so as to achieve a balance between anthropogenic emissions by sources and removals by sinks of greenhouse gases in the

second half of this century, on the basis of equity, and in the context of sustainable development and efforts to eradicate poverty.

2. Each Party shall prepare, communicate and maintain successive nationally determined contributions that it intends to achieve. Parties shall pursue domestic mitigation measures, with the aim of achieving the objectives of such contributions.

3. Each Party's successive nationally determined contribution will represent a progression beyond the Party's then current nationally determined contribution and reflect its highest possible ambition, reflecting its common but differentiated responsibilities and respective capabilities, in the light of different national circumstances.

4. Developed country Parties should continue taking the lead by undertaking economy-wide absolute emission reduction targets. Developing country Parties should continue enhancing their mitigation efforts, and are encouraged to move over time towards economy-wide emission reduction or limitation targets in the light of different national circumstances.

5. Support shall be provided to developing country Parties for the implementation of this Article, in accordance with Articles 9, 10 and 11, recognizing that enhanced support for developing country Parties will allow for higher ambition in their actions.

6. The least developed countries and small island developing States may prepare and communicate strategies, plans and actions for low greenhouse gas emissions development reflecting their special circumstances.

7. Mitigation co-benefits resulting from Parties' adaptation actions and/or economic diversification plans can contribute to mitigation outcomes under this Article.

8. In communicating their nationally determined contributions, all Parties shall provide the information necessary for clarity, transparency and understanding in accordance with decision 1/CP.21 and any relevant decisions of the Conference of the Parties serving as the meeting of the Parties to the Paris Agreement.

9. Each Party shall communicate a nationally determined contribution every five years in accordance with decision 1/CP.21 and any relevant decisions of the Conference of the Parties serving as the meeting of the Parties to the Paris Agreement and be informed by the outcomes of the global stocktake referred to in Article 14.

10. The Conference of the Parties serving as the meeting of the Parties to the Paris Agreement shall consider common time frames for nationally determined contributions at its first session.

11. A Party may at any time adjust its existing nationally determined contribution with a view to enhancing its level of ambition, in accordance with guidance adopted by the Conference of the Parties serving as the meeting of the Parties to the Paris Agreement.

12. Nationally determined contributions communicated by Parties shall be recorded in a public registry maintained by the secretariat.

13. Parties shall account for their nationally determined contributions. In accounting for anthropogenic emissions and removals

corresponding to their nationally determined contributions, Parties shall promote environmental integrity, transparency, accuracy, completeness, comparability and consistency, and ensure the avoidance of double counting, in accordance with guidance adopted by the Conference of the Parties serving as the meeting of the Parties to the Paris Agreement.

14.   In the context of their nationally determined contributions, when recognizing and implementing mitigation actions with respect to anthropogenic emissions and removals, Parties should take into account, as appropriate, existing methods and guidance under the Convention, in the light of the provisions of paragraph 13 of this Article.

15.   Parties shall take into consideration in the implementation of this Agreement the concerns of Parties with economies most affected by the impacts of response measures, particularly developing country Parties.

16.   Parties, including regional economic integration organizations and their member States, that have reached an agreement to act jointly under paragraph 2 of this Article shall notify the secretariat of the terms of that agreement, including the emission level allocated to each Party within the relevant time period, when they communicate their nationally determined contributions. The secretariat shall in turn inform the Parties and signatories to the Convention of the terms of that agreement.

17.   Each party to such an agreement shall be responsible for its emission level as set out in the agreement referred to in paragraph 16 above in accordance with paragraphs 13 and 14 of this

Article and Articles 13 and 15.

18.   If Parties acting jointly do so in the framework of, and together with, a regional economic integration organization which is itself a Party to this Agreement, each member State of that regional economic integration organization individually, and together with the regional economic integration organization, shall be responsible for its emission level as set out in the agreement communicated under paragraph 16 of this Article in accordance with paragraphs 13 and 14 of this Article and Articles 13 and 15.

19.   All Parties should strive to formulate and communicate long-term low greenhouse gas emission development strategies, mindful of Article 2 taking into account their common but differentiated responsibilities and respective capabilities, in the light of different national circumstances.

Article 5

1. Parties should take action to conserve and enhance, as appropriate, sinks and reservoirs of greenhouse gases as referred to in Article 4, paragraph 1(d), of the Convention, including forests.

2. Parties are encouraged to take action to implement and support, including through results-based payments, the existing framework as set out in related guidance and decisions already agreed under the Convention for: policy approaches and positive incentives for activities relating to reducing emissions from deforestation and forest degradation, and the role of conservation, sustainable management of forests and enhancement of forest carbon stocks in developing countries; and alternative policy

approaches, such as joint mitigation and adaptation approaches for the integral and sustainable management of forests, while reaffirming the importance of incentivizing, as appropriate, non-carbon benefits associated with such approaches.

Article 6

1. Parties recognize that some Parties choose to pursue voluntary cooperation in the implementation of their nationally determined contributions to allow for higher ambition in their mitigation and adaptation actions and to promote sustainable development and environmental integrity.

2. Parties shall, where engaging on a voluntary basis in cooperative approaches that involve the use of internationally transferred mitigation outcomes towards nationally determined contributions, promote sustainable development and ensure environmental integrity and transparency, including in governance, and shall apply robust accounting to ensure, inter alia, the avoidance of double counting, consistent with guidance adopted by the Conference of the Parties serving as the meeting of the Parties to the Paris Agreement.

3. The use of internationally transferred mitigation outcomes to achieve nationally determined contributions under this Agreement shall be voluntary and authorized by participating Parties.

4. A mechanism to contribute to the mitigation of greenhouse gas emissions and support sustainable development is hereby established under the authority and guidance of the Conference of the Parties serving as the meeting of the Parties to the Paris Agreement for use by Parties on a voluntary basis. It shall be supervised by a body designated

by the Conference of the Parties serving as the meeting of the Parties to the Paris Agreement, and shall aim:

.
   (a) To promote the mitigation of greenhouse gas emissions while fostering sustainable development;

.
   (b) To incentivize and facilitate participation in the mitigation of greenhouse gas emissions by public and private entities authorized by a Party;

.
   (c) To contribute to the reduction of emission levels in the host Party, which will benefit from mitigation activities resulting in emission reductions that can also be used by another Party to fulfil its nationally determined contribution; and

.
   (d) To deliver an overall mitigation in global emissions.

5. Emission reductions resulting from the mechanism referred to in paragraph 4 of this Article shall not be used to demonstrate achievement of the host Party's nationally determined contribution if used by another Party to demonstrate achievement of its nationally determined contribution.

6. The Conference of the Parties serving as the meeting of the Parties to the Paris Agreement shall ensure that a share of the proceeds from activities under the mechanism referred to in paragraph 4 of this Article is used to cover administrative expenses as well as to assist developing country Parties that are particularly vulnerable to the adverse effects of climate change to meet the costs of adaptation.

7. The Conference of the Parties serving as the meeting of the Parties to the Paris Agreement shall adopt rules, modalities and procedures for the mechanism referred to in paragraph 4 of this Article at its first session.

8. Parties recognize the importance of integrated, holistic and balanced non-market approaches being available to Parties to assist in the implementation of their nationally determined contributions, in the context of sustainable development and poverty eradication, in a coordinated and effective manner, including through, inter alia, mitigation, adaptation, finance, technology transfer and capacity-building, as appropriate. These approaches shall aim to:

.   (a) Promote mitigation and adaptation ambition;

.   (b) Enhance public and private sector participation in the implementation of nationally determined contributions; and

.   (c) Enable opportunities for coordination across instruments and relevant institutional arrangements.

9. A framework for non-market approaches to sustainable development is hereby defined to promote the non- market approaches referred to in paragraph 8 of this Article.

Article 7

1. Parties hereby establish the global goal on adaptation of enhancing adaptive capacity, strengthening resilience and reducing vulnerability to climate change, with a view to contributing to sustainable development and ensuring an adequate adaptation response in the context of the temperature goal

referred to in Article 2.

2. Parties recognize that adaptation is a global challenge faced by all with local, subnational, national, regional and international dimensions, and that it is a key component of and makes a contribution to the long-term global response to climate change to protect people, livelihoods and ecosystems, taking into account the urgent and immediate needs of those developing country Parties that are particularly vulnerable to the adverse effects of climate change.

3. The adaptation efforts of developing country Parties shall be recognized, in accordance with the modalities to be adopted by the Conference of the Parties serving as the meeting of the Parties to the Paris Agreement at its first session.

4. Parties recognize that the current need for adaptation is significant and that greater levels of mitigation can reduce the need for additional adaptation efforts, and that greater adaptation needs can involve greater adaptation costs.

5. Parties acknowledge that adaptation action should follow a country-driven, gender-responsive, participatory and fully transparent approach, taking into consideration vulnerable groups, communities and ecosystems, and should be based on and guided by the best available science and, as appropriate, traditional knowledge, knowledge of indigenous peoples and local knowledge systems, with a view to integrating adaptation into relevant socioeconomic and environmental policies and actions, where appropriate.

6. Parties recognize the importance of support for and international cooperation on adaptation efforts and the importance of taking into account the needs of

developing country Parties, especially those that are particularly vulnerable to the adverse effects of climate change.

7. Parties should strengthen their cooperation on enhancing action on adaptation, taking into account the Cancun Adaptation Framework, including with regard to:

.   (a) Sharing information, good practices, experiences and lessons learned, including, as appropriate, as these relate to science, planning, policies and implementation in relation to adaptation actions;

.   (b) Strengthening institutional arrangements, including those under the Convention that serve this Agreement, to support the synthesis of relevant information and knowledge, and the provision of technical support and guidance to Parties;

.   (c) Strengthening scientific knowledge on climate, including research, systematic observation of the climate system and early warning systems, in a manner that informs climate services and supports decision- making;

.   (d) Assisting developing country Parties in identifying effective adaptation practices, adaptation needs, priorities, support provided and received for adaptation actions and efforts, and challenges and gaps, in a manner consistent with encouraging good practices;

.   (e) Improving the effectiveness and durability of adaptation actions.

8. United Nations specialized organizations and agencies are encouraged to support the efforts of Parties to implement the actions referred to in paragraph 7 of this Article, taking into account the provisions of paragraph 5 of this Article.

9. Each Party shall, as appropriate, engage in adaptation planning processes and the implementation of actions, including the development or enhancement of relevant plans, policies and/or contributions, which may include:

.   (a) The implementation of adaptation actions, undertakings and/or efforts;

.   (b) The process to formulate and implement national adaptation plans;

.   (c) The assessment of climate change impacts and vulnerability, with a view to formulating nationally determined prioritized actions, taking into account vulnerable people, places and ecosystems;

.   (d) Monitoring and evaluating and learning from adaptation plans, policies, programmes and actions; and

.   (e) Building the resilience of socioeconomic and ecological systems, including through economic diversification and sustainable management of natural resources.

10.   Each Party should, as appropriate, submit and update periodically an adaptation communication, which may include its priorities, implementation and support needs, plans and actions, without creating any additional burden for developing

country Parties.

11. The adaptation communication referred to in paragraph 10 of this Article shall be, as appropriate, submitted and updated periodically, as a component of or in conjunction with other communications or documents, including a national adaptation plan, a nationally determined contribution as referred to in Article 4, paragraph 2, and/or a national communication.

12. The adaptation communications referred to in paragraph 10 of this Article shall be recorded in a public registry maintained by the secretariat.

13. Continuous and enhanced international support shall be provided to developing country Parties for the implementation of paragraphs 7, 9, 10 and 11 of this Article, in accordance with the provisions of Articles 9, 10 and 11.

14. The global stocktake referred to in Article 14 shall, inter alia:

    (a) Recognize adaptation efforts of developing country Parties;

    (b) Enhance the implementation of adaptation action taking into account the adaptation communication referred to in paragraph 10 of this Article;

    (c) Review the adequacy and effectiveness of adaptation and support provided for adaptation; and

    (d) Review the overall progress made in achieving the global goal on adaptation referred to in paragraph 1 of this Article.

Article 8

1. Parties recognize the importance of averting, minimizing and addressing loss and damage associated with the adverse effects of climate change, including extreme weather events and slow onset events, and the role of sustainable development in reducing the risk of loss and damage.

2. The Warsaw International Mechanism for Loss and Damage associated with Climate Change Impacts shall be subject to the authority and guidance of the Conference of the Parties serving as the meeting of the Parties to the Paris Agreement and may be enhanced and strengthened, as determined by the Conference of the Parties serving as the meeting of the Parties to the Paris Agreement.

3. Parties should enhance understanding, action and support, including through the Warsaw International Mechanism, as appropriate, on a cooperative and facilitative basis with respect to loss and damage associated with the adverse effects of climate change.

4. Accordingly, areas of cooperation and facilitation to enhance understanding, action and support may include:

.   (a) Early warning systems;

.   (b) Emergency preparedness;

.   (c) Slow onset events;

.   (d) Events that may involve irreversible and permanent loss and damage;

.   (e) Comprehensive risk assessment and management;

.   (f) Risk insurance facilities, climate risk

pooling and other insurance solutions;

.   (g) Non-economic losses;

.   (h) Resilience of communities, livelihoods and ecosystems.

5. The Warsaw International Mechanism shall collaborate with existing bodies and expert groups under the Agreement, as well as relevant organizations and expert bodies outside the Agreement.

Article 9

1. Developed country Parties shall provide financial resources to assist developing country Parties with respect to both mitigation and adaptation in continuation of their existing obligations under the Convention.

2. Other Parties are encouraged to provide or continue to provide such support voluntarily.

3. As part of a global effort, developed country Parties should continue to take the lead in mobilizing climate finance from a wide variety of sources, instruments and channels, noting the significant role of public funds, through a variety of actions, including supporting country-driven strategies, and taking into account the needs and priorities of developing country Parties. Such mobilization of climate finance should represent a progression beyond previous efforts.

4. The provision of scaled-up financial resources should aim to achieve a balance between adaptation and mitigation, taking into account country-driven strategies, and the priorities and needs of developing country Parties, especially those that are particularly vulnerable to the adverse effects of climate change and have significant capacity

constraints, such as the least developed countries and small island developing States, considering the need for public and grant-based resources for adaptation.

5. Developed country Parties shall biennially communicate indicative quantitative and qualitative information related to paragraphs 1 and 3 of this Article, as applicable, including, as available, projected levels of public financial resources to be provided to developing country Parties. Other Parties providing resources are encouraged to communicate biennially such information on a voluntary basis.

6. The global stocktake referred to in Article 14 shall take into account the relevant information provided by developed country Parties and/or Agreement bodies on efforts related to climate finance.

7. Developed country Parties shall provide transparent and consistent information on support for developing country Parties provided and mobilized through public interventions biennially in accordance with the modalities, procedures and guidelines to be adopted by the Conference of the Parties serving as the meeting of the Parties to the Paris Agreement, at its first session, as stipulated in Article 13, paragraph 13. Other Parties are encouraged to do so.

8. The Financial Mechanism of the Convention, including its operating entities, shall serve as the financial mechanism of this Agreement.

9. The institutions serving this Agreement, including the operating entities of the Financial Mechanism of the Convention, shall aim to ensure efficient access to financial resources through simplified approval procedures and enhanced readiness

support for developing country Parties, in particular for the least developed countries and small island developing States, in the context of their national climate strategies and plans.

Article 10

1. Parties share a long-term vision on the importance of fully realizing technology development and transfer in order to improve resilience to climate change and to reduce greenhouse gas emissions.

2. Parties, noting the importance of technology for the implementation of mitigation and adaptation actions under this Agreement and recognizing existing technology deployment and dissemination efforts, shall strengthen cooperative action on technology development and transfer.

3. The Technology Mechanism established under the Convention shall serve this Agreement.

4. A technology framework is hereby established to provide overarching guidance to the work of the Technology Mechanism in promoting and facilitating enhanced action on technology development and transfer in order to support the implementation of this Agreement, in pursuit of the long-term vision referred to in paragraph 1 of this Article.

5. Accelerating, encouraging and enabling innovation is critical for an effective, long-term global response to climate change and promoting economic growth and sustainable development. Such effort shall be, as appropriate, supported, including by the Technology Mechanism and, through financial means, by the Financial Mechanism of the Convention, for collaborative approaches to

research and development, and facilitating access to technology, in particular for early stages of the technology cycle, to developing country Parties.

6. Support, including financial support, shall be provided to developing country Parties for the implementation of this Article, including for strengthening cooperative action on technology development and transfer at different stages of the technology cycle, with a view to achieving a balance between support for mitigation and adaptation. The global stocktake referred to in Article 14 shall take into account available information on efforts related to support on technology development and transfer for developing country Parties.

Article 11

1. Capacity-building under this Agreement should enhance the capacity and ability of developing country Parties, in particular countries with the least capacity, such as the least developed countries, and those that are particularly vulnerable to the adverse effects of climate change, such as small island developing States, to take effective climate change action, including, inter alia, to implement adaptation and mitigation actions, and should facilitate technology development, dissemination and deployment, access to climate finance, relevant aspects of education, training and public awareness, and the transparent, timely and accurate communication of information.

2. Capacity-building should be country-driven, based on and responsive to national needs, and foster country ownership of Parties, in particular, for developing country Parties, including at the

national, subnational and local levels. Capacity-building should be guided by lessons learned, including those from capacity-building activities under the Convention, and should be an effective, iterative process that is participatory, cross-cutting and gender-responsive.

3. All Parties should cooperate to enhance the capacity of developing country Parties to implement this Agreement. Developed country Parties should enhance support for capacity-building actions in developing country Parties.

4. All Parties enhancing the capacity of developing country Parties to implement this Agreement, including through regional, bilateral and multilateral approaches, shall regularly communicate on these actions or measures on capacity-building. Developing country Parties should regularly communicate progress made on implementing capacity-building plans, policies, actions or measures to implement this Agreement.

5. Capacity-building activities shall be enhanced through appropriate institutional arrangements to support the implementation of this Agreement, including the appropriate institutional arrangements established under the Convention that serve this Agreement. The Conference of the Parties serving as the meeting of the Parties to the Paris Agreement shall, at its first session, consider and adopt a decision on the initial institutional arrangements for capacity-building.

Article 12

Parties shall cooperate in taking measures, as appropriate, to enhance climate change education, training, public awareness, public participation and public access to information, recognizing the importance of these steps with respect to enhancing actions under this Agreement.

Article 13

1. In order to build mutual trust and confidence and to promote effective implementation, an enhanced transparency framework for action and support, with built-in flexibility which takes into account Parties' different capacities and builds upon collective experience is hereby established.

2. The transparency framework shall provide flexibility in the implementation of the provisions of this Article to those developing country Parties that need it in the light of their capacities. The modalities, procedures and guidelines referred to in paragraph 13 of this Article shall reflect such flexibility.

3. The transparency framework shall build on and enhance the transparency arrangements under the Convention, recognizing the special circumstances of the least developed countries and small island developing States, and be implemented in a facilitative, non-intrusive, non-punitive manner, respectful of national sovereignty, and avoid placing undue burden on Parties.

4. The transparency arrangements under the Convention, including national communications, biennial reports and biennial update reports, international assessment and review and international consultation and analysis, shall form part of the experience drawn upon for the development of the modalities, procedures and guidelines under paragraph 13 of this Article.

5. The purpose of the framework for transparency of

action is to provide a clear understanding of climate change action in the light of the objective of the Convention as set out in its Article 2, including clarity and tracking of progress towards achieving Parties' individual nationally determined contributions under Article 4, and Parties' adaptation actions under Article 7, including good practices, priorities, needs and gaps, to inform the global stocktake under Article 14.

6. The purpose of the framework for transparency of support is to provide clarity on support provided and received by relevant individual Parties in the context of climate change actions under Articles 4, 7, 9, 10 and 11, and, to the extent possible, to provide a full overview of aggregate financial support provided, to inform the global stocktake under Article 14.

7. Each Party shall regularly provide the following information:

. (a) A national inventory report of anthropogenic emissions by sources and removals by sinks of greenhouse gases, prepared using good practice methodologies accepted by the Intergovernmental Panel on Climate Change and agreed upon by the Conference of the Parties serving as the meeting of the Parties to the Paris Agreement;

. (b) Information necessary to track progress made in implementing and achieving its nationally determined contribution under Article 4.

8. Each Party should also provide information related to climate change impacts and adaptation under Article 7, as appropriate.

9. Developed country Parties shall, and other Parties that provide support should, provide information on

financial, technology transfer and capacity-building support provided to developing country Parties under Article 9, 10 and 11.

10. Developing country Parties should provide information on financial, technology transfer and capacity-building support needed and received under Articles 9, 10 and 11.

11. Information submitted by each Party under paragraphs 7 and 9 of this Article shall undergo a technical expert review, in accordance with decision 1/CP.21. For those developing country Parties that need it in the light of their capacities, the review process shall include assistance in identifying capacity-building needs. In addition, each Party shall participate in a facilitative, multilateral consideration of progress with respect to efforts under Article 9, and its respective implementation and achievement of its nationally determined contribution.

12. The technical expert review under this paragraph shall consist of a consideration of the Party's support provided, as relevant, and its implementation and achievement of its nationally determined contribution. The review shall also identify areas of improvement for the Party, and include a review of the consistency of the information with the modalities, procedures and guidelines referred to in paragraph 13 of this Article, taking into account the flexibility accorded to the Party under paragraph 2 of this Article. The review shall pay particular attention to the respective national capabilities and circumstances of developing country Parties.

13. The Conference of the Parties serving as the meeting of the Parties to the Paris Agreement shall, at its first session, building on experience

from the arrangements related to transparency under the Convention, and elaborating on the provisions in this Article, adopt common modalities, procedures and guidelines, as appropriate, for the transparency of action and support.

14. Support shall be provided to developing countries for the implementation of this Article.

15. Support shall also be provided for the building of transparency-related capacity of developing country Parties on a continuous basis.

Article 14

1. The Conference of the Parties serving as the meeting of the Parties to the Paris Agreement shall periodically take stock of the implementation of this Agreement to assess the collective progress towards achieving the purpose of this Agreement and its long-term goals (referred to as the "global stocktake"). It shall do so in a comprehensive and facilitative manner, considering mitigation, adaptation and the means of implementation and support, and in the light of equity and the best available science.

2. The Conference of the Parties serving as the meeting of the Parties to the Paris Agreement shall undertake its first global stocktake in 2023 and every five years thereafter unless otherwise decided by the Conference of the Parties serving as the meeting of the Parties to the Paris Agreement.

3. The outcome of the global stocktake shall inform Parties in updating and enhancing, in a nationally determined manner, their actions and support in accordance with the relevant provisions of this Agreement, as well as in enhancing international

cooperation for climate action.

Article 15

1. A mechanism to facilitate implementation of and
     promote compliance with the provisions of this
     Agreement is hereby established.

2. The mechanism referred to in paragraph 1 of this
     Article shall consist of a committee that shall be
     expert-based and facilitative in nature and
     function in a manner that is transparent, non-
     adversarial and non-punitive. The committee shall
     pay particular attention to the respective national
     capabilities and circumstances of Parties.

3. The committee shall operate under the modalities and
procedures adopted by the Conference of the Parties
serving as the meeting of the Parties to the Paris
Agreement at its first session and report annually to the
Conference of the Parties serving as the meeting of the
Parties to the Paris Agreement.

Article 16

1. The Conference of the Parties, the supreme body of the
     Convention, shall serve as the meeting of the
     Parties to this Agreement.

2. Parties to the Convention that are not Parties to this
     Agreement may participate as observers in the
     proceedings of any session of the Conference of
     the Parties serving as the meeting of the Parties to
     this Agreement. When the Conference of the
     Parties serves as the meeting of the Parties to this
     Agreement, decisions under this Agreement shall
     be taken only by those that are Parties to this
     Agreement.

3. When the Conference of the Parties serves as the meeting of the Parties to this Agreement, any member of the Bureau of the Conference of the Parties representing a Party to the Convention but, at that time, not a Party to this Agreement, shall be replaced by an additional member to be elected by and from amongst the Parties to this Agreement.

4. The Conference of the Parties serving as the meeting of the Parties to the Paris Agreement shall keep under regular review the implementation of this Agreement and shall make, within its mandate, the decisions necessary to promote its effective implementation. It shall perform the functions assigned to it by this Agreement and shall:

  (a) Establish such subsidiary bodies as deemed necessary for the implementation of this Agreement; and

  (b) Exercise such other functions as may be required for the implementation of this Agreement.

5. The rules of procedure of the Conference of the Parties and the financial procedures applied under the Convention shall be applied mutatis mutandis under this Agreement, except as may be otherwise decided by consensus by the Conference of the Parties serving as the meeting of the Parties to the Paris Agreement.

6. The first session of the Conference of the Parties serving as the meeting of the Parties to the Paris Agreement shall be convened by the secretariat in conjunction with the first session of the Conference of the Parties that is scheduled after the date of entry into force of this Agreement. Subsequent ordinary sessions of the Conference of

the Parties serving as the meeting of the Parties to the Paris Agreement shall be held in conjunction with ordinary sessions of the Conference of the Parties, unless otherwise decided by the Conference of the Parties serving as the meeting of the Parties to the Paris Agreement.

7. Extraordinary sessions of the Conference of the Parties serving as the meeting of the Parties to the Paris Agreement shall be held at such other times as may be deemed necessary by the Conference of the Parties serving as the meeting of the Parties to the Paris Agreement or at the written request of any Party, provided that, within six months of the request being communicated to the Parties by the secretariat, it is supported by at least one third of the Parties.

8. The United Nations and its specialized agencies and the International Atomic Energy Agency, as well as any State member thereof or observers thereto not party to the Convention, may be represented at sessions of the Conference of the Parties serving as the meeting of the Parties to the Paris Agreement as observers. Any body or agency, whether national or international, governmental or non-governmental, which is qualified in matters covered by this Agreement and which has informed the secretariat of its wish to be represented at a session of the Conference of the Parties serving as the meeting of the Parties to the Paris Agreement as an observer, may be so admitted unless at least one third of the Parties present object. The admission and participation of observers shall be subject to the rules of procedure referred to in paragraph 5 of this Article.

Article 17

1. The secretariat established by Article 8 of the

Convention shall serve as the secretariat of this Agreement.

2. Article 8, paragraph 2, of the Convention on the functions of the secretariat, and Article 8, paragraph 3, of the Convention, on the arrangements made for the functioning of the secretariat, shall apply mutatis mutandis to this Agreement. The secretariat shall, in addition, exercise the functions assigned to it under this Agreement and by the Conference of the Parties serving as the meeting of the Parties to the Paris Agreement.

Article 18

1. The Subsidiary Body for Scientific and Technological Advice and the Subsidiary Body for Implementation established by Articles 9 and 10 of the Convention shall serve, respectively, as the Subsidiary Body for Scientific and Technological Advice and the Subsidiary Body for Implementation of this Agreement. The provisions of the Convention relating to the functioning of these two bodies shall apply mutatis mutandis to this Agreement. Sessions of the meetings of the Subsidiary Body for Scientific and Technological Advice and the Subsidiary Body for Implementation of this Agreement shall be held in conjunction with the meetings of, respectively, the Subsidiary Body for Scientific and Technological Advice and the Subsidiary Body for Implementation of the Convention.

2. Parties to the Convention that are not Parties to this Agreement may participate as observers in the proceedings of any session of the subsidiary bodies. When the subsidiary bodies serve as the subsidiary bodies of this Agreement, decisions under this Agreement shall be taken only by those

that are Parties to this Agreement.

3. When the subsidiary bodies established by Articles 9 and 10 of the Convention exercise their functions with regard to matters concerning this Agreement, any member of the bureaux of those subsidiary bodies representing a Party to the Convention but, at that time, not a Party to this Agreement, shall be replaced by an additional member to be elected by and from amongst the Parties to this Agreement.

Article 19

1. Subsidiary bodies or other institutional arrangements established by or under the Convention, other than those referred to in this Agreement, shall serve this Agreement upon a decision of the Conference of the Parties serving as the meeting of the Parties to the Paris Agreement. The Conference of the Parties serving as the meeting of the Parties to the Paris Agreement shall specify the functions to be exercised by such subsidiary bodies or arrangements.

2. The Conference of the Parties serving as the meeting of the Parties to the Paris Agreement may provide further guidance to such subsidiary bodies and institutional arrangements.

Article 20

1. This Agreement shall be open for signature and subject to ratification, acceptance or approval by States and regional economic integration organizations that are Parties to the Convention. It shall be open for signature at the United Nations Headquarters in New York from 22 April 2016 to 21 April 2017. Thereafter, this Agreement shall be open for accession from the day following the date on

which it is closed for signature. Instruments of ratification, acceptance, approval or accession shall be deposited with the Depositary.

2. Any regional economic integration organization that becomes a Party to this Agreement without any of its member States being a Party shall be bound by all the obligations under this Agreement. In the case of regional economic integration organizations with one or more member States that are Parties to this Agreement, the organization and its member States shall decide on their respective responsibilities for the performance of their obligations under this Agreement. In such cases, the organization and the member States shall not be entitled to exercise rights under this Agreement concurrently.

3. In their instruments of ratification, acceptance, approval or accession, regional economic integration organizations shall declare the extent of their competence with respect to the matters governed by this Agreement. These organizations shall also inform the Depositary, who shall in turn inform the Parties, of any substantial modification in the extent of their competence.

Article 21

1. This Agreement shall enter into force on the thirtieth day after the date on which at least 55 Parties to the Convention accounting in total for at least an estimated 55 percent of the total global greenhouse gas emissions have deposited their instruments of ratification, acceptance, approval or accession.

2. Solely for the limited purpose of paragraph 1 of this Article, "total global greenhouse gas emissions" means the most up-to-date amount communicated

on or before the date of adoption of this
Agreement by the Parties to the Convention.

3. For each State or regional economic integration
organization that ratifies, accepts or approves this
Agreement or accedes thereto after the conditions
set out in paragraph 1 of this Article for entry into
force have been fulfilled, this Agreement shall
enter into force on the thirtieth day after the date
of deposit by such State or regional economic
integration organization of its instrument of
ratification, acceptance, approval or accession.

4. For the purposes of paragraph 1 of this Article, any
instrument deposited by a regional economic integration
organization shall not be counted as additional to those
deposited by its member States.

Article 22

The provisions of Article 15 of the Convention on the
adoption of amendments to the Convention shall apply
mutatis mutandis to this Agreement.

Article 23

1. The provisions of Article 16 of the Convention on the
adoption and amendment of annexes to the
Convention shall apply mutatis mutandis to this
Agreement.

2. Annexes to this Agreement shall form an integral part
thereof and, unless otherwise expressly provided
for, a reference to this Agreement constitutes at
the same time a reference to any annexes thereto.
Such annexes shall be restricted to lists, forms and
any other material of a descriptive nature that is of
a scientific, technical, procedural or administrative
character.

Article 24

The provisions of Article 14 of the Convention on settlement of disputes shall apply mutatis mutandis to this Agreement.

Article 25

1. Each Party shall have one vote, except as provided for paragraph 2 of this Article.

2. Regional economic integration organizations, in matters within their competence, shall exercise their right to vote with a number of votes equal to the number of their member States that are Parties to this Agreement. Such an organization shall not exercise its right to vote if any of its member States exercises its right, and vice versa.

Article 26

The Secretary-General of the United Nations shall be the Depositary of this Agreement.

Article 27

No reservations may be made to this Agreement.

Article 28

1. At any time after three years from the date on which this Agreement has entered into force for a Party, that Party may withdraw from this Agreement by giving written notification to the Depositary.

2. Any such withdrawal shall take effect upon expiry of one year from the date of receipt by the Depositary of the notification of withdrawal, or on such later date as may be specified in the notification of withdrawal.

3. Any Party that withdraws from the Convention shall be considered as also having withdrawn from this

Agreement.

Article 29

The original of this Agreement, of which the Arabic, Chinese, English, French, Russian and Spanish texts are equally authentic, shall be deposited with the Secretary-General of the United Nations.

DONE at Paris this twelfth day of December two thousand and fifteen.   IN WITNESS WHEREOF, the undersigned, being duly authorized to that effect, have signed this Agreement.

References

Abbot, John; James Delingpole, Robert M. Carter; Rupert Darwall; Donna Laframboise, Christopher Essex; Stewart W. Franks Kesten C. Green; Richard S. Lindzen, Nigel Lawson; Bernard Lewin; Patrick J. Michaels; Alan Moran, Jennifer Marohasy Ross McKitrick ; Nova, Jo; Willie Soon, Garth W. Paltridge; Ian Plimer; Steyn, Mark; Watts, Anthony; Andrew Bolt; J. Scott Armstrong. 2015. *Climate Change: The Facts*. Stockade Books. Kindle Edition.

Alley, Richard B. 2014. *The Two-Mile Time Machine: Ice Cores, Abrupt Climate Change, and Our Future*. Princeton University Press. Kindle Edition.

Bell, Larry. 2015. *Scared Witless: Prophets and Profits of Climate Doom*. Stairway Press. Kindle Edition.

Biermann, Frank. 2014. *Earth System Governance: World Politics in the Anthropocene*. MIT Press

Brooke, John L. 2014. *Climate Change and the Course of Global History*. Cambridge University Press.

Carlin, Alan. 2015. *Environmentalism Gone Mad: How a Sierra Club Activist and Senior EPA Analyst Discovered a Radical Green Energy Fantasy*. Stairway Press. Kindle Edition.

Chasek, Pamela S. David L. Downie and Janet Welsh Brown. 2013. *Global Environmental Politics (Dilemmas in World Politics)*. Westview Press; Sixth Edition.

Christoff, Peter; Eckersley, Robyn. 2013. *Globalization and the Environment*. Rowman & Littlefield Publishers. Kindle Edition.

Compston, Hugh; Bailey, Ian. 2013. *Climate Clever: How Governments Can Tackle Climate Change (and Still Win Elections).* Taylor and Francis. Kindle Edition.

Cushman, John H. 2014. *Keystone and Beyond: Tar Sands and the National Interest in the Era of Climate Change.* Amazon/Kindle.

DiMento, Joseph F.C.; Doughman, Pamela. 2014. *Climate Change: What It Means for Us, Our Children, and Our Grandchildren* (American and Comparative Environmental Policy). The MIT Press. Kindle Edition.

Fensin, Alan. 2015. *The Global Warming, Carbon Dioxide Hoax: Easy to Read Proof That Climate Change Is Normal and Not Man-Made.* Burlington National Inc.. Kindle Edition.

Greer, John Michael. 2011. *The Wealth of Nature: Economics as if Survival Mattered.* New Society Publishers. Kindle Edition.

Griffin, David Ray. 2015. *Unprecedented: Can Civilization Survive the CO2 Crisis.* Clarity Press, Kindle Edition.

Hansen, James, 2009, *Storms of My Grandchildren,* Bloomsberry.

Hertsgaard, Mark, 2011, *Hot: Living through the next Fifty Years on Earth,* Houghton Mifflin Harcourt

Heck, Stevan and Matt Rogers. 2014. *Resource Revolution.* Amazon/Kindle.

Heinberg, Richard. 2015. *Afterburn: Society Beyond Fossil Fuels.* New Society Publishers. Kindle Edition.

Howe, Joshua P. 2014. *Behind the Curve: Science and the Politics of Global Warming* (Weyerhaeuser Environmental Books). University of Washington Press. Kindle Edition.

IPCC: Intergovernmental Panel on Climate Change. 2013-14. *Fifth Assessment Report.* ipcc.int NOTE: the report has two publication dates because the science section was published in 2013 and the impacts and policies sections were published in 2014.

Klein, Naomi. 2014. *This Changes Everything: Capitalism vs. The Climate.* Simon & Schuster.

McGraw, Seamus. 2015. *Betting the Farm on a Drought: Stories from the Front Lines of Climate Change.* University of Texas Press. Kindle Edition.

McPherson, William. 2014. *Ideology Versus Science.* Amazon/Kindle.

McPherson, William. 2015. *Climate, Weather and Ideology.* Amazon/Kindle.

Michaels, Patrick J.; Knappenberger, Paul C. 2015. *Lukewarming: The New Climate Science that Changes Everything.* Kindle Edition.

Pickett, Kate; Wilkinson, Richard. 2010. *The Spirit Level.* Bloomsbury Publishing Plc. Kindle Edition.

Romm, Joseph. 2015. *Climate Change: What Everyone Needs to Know.* Oxford University Press. Kindle Edition.

Smith, Philip; Howe, Nicolas. 2015. *Climate Change as Social Drama: Global Warming in the Public Sphere.* Cambridge University Press. Kindle Edition.

Stern, Nicholas. 2015. *Why Are We Waiting?: The Logic, Urgency, and Promise of Tackling Climate Change (Lionel Robbins Lectures).* The MIT Press. Kindle Edition.

Stephenson, Wen. 2015. *What We're Fighting for Now Is Each Other: Dispatches from the Front Lines of Climate Justice.* Beacon Press.

Stevenson, Haley and John S. Dryzek. 2014. *Democratizing Global Climate Governance.* Cambridge University Press

Talbott, Strobe; Antholis, William. 2011. *Fast Forward: Ethics and Politics in the Age of Global Warming* (Brookings FOCUS Book). Brookings Institution Press. Kindle Edition.

Vince, Gaia. 2014. *Adventures in the Anthropocene: A Journey to the Heart of the Planet We Made*. Milkweed Editions. Kindle Edition.

Welzer, Harald. 2015. *Climate Wars: What People Will Be Killed For in the 21st Century.* Wiley. Kindle Edition

Wood, Mary Christina. 2013. *Nature's Trust*. Cambridge University Press. Kindle Edition.

Notes

1 McPherson, 2014.

2
http://unfccc.int/files/essential_background/background_
publications_htmlpdf/application/pdf/conveng.pdf

3 *Guardian,* November 9, 2015.

4 One author has summarized the research as follows: "The generally conservative IEA affirmed that at least two-thirds of proven fossil-fuel reserves must stay in the ground, between then and 2050, in order to have a shot at keeping the global average temperature from rising more than two degrees Celsius, the internationally agreed-upon "red line." Meanwhile, as we've seen, the World Bank warned that the planet is on track for a four-degree-Celsius rise this century— which it said "must be avoided." The analysts at PwC, in a report titled Too Late for Two Degrees?, concluded that we've "passed a critical threshold," and should prepare for four degrees, or even six degrees, this century, unless the carbon-intensity of the global economy can be reduced by an unprecedented 5 percent per year for the next forty years." Stephenson, 2015.

5 Rtcc.org, May 4, 2015.The Grantham Research Institute on Climate Change and the Environment is a research center at the London School of Economics.

6 Scholarly studies have attributed to Kyoto an apocalyptic significance: "This apocalyptic discourse of global doom set high popular expectations for the 1997 meetings in Kyoto. There were vague hopes for a potlatch ceremony of selfless action in which national interests would be thrown over the cliff. This ritual validation of the apocalyptic worldview might, some hoped, provide the foundation point for a new romantic narrative, one involving sacrifice, sharing, and the pursuit of a common good." Smith and Howe, 2015.

7 Reuters, October 12, 2015.

8 Ibid. This is a quote from Yvo de Boer, former Executive Director of UNFCCC.

9 Some have reacted in kind. Senator Ted Cruz (R-TX), a candidate for president, said "On the global warming alarmists, anyone who actually points to the evidence that disproves their apocalyptical claims, they don't engage in reasoned debate. What do they do? They scream, 'You're a denier.' They brand you a heretic. Today, the global warming alarmists are the equivalent of the flat-Earthers. It used to be [that] it is accepted scientific wisdom the Earth is flat, and this heretic named Galileo was branded a denier." *Washington Post,* March 25, 2015. Cruz is somewhat off base in his science history: Galileo was condemned for claiming that the earth revolved around the sun, not because he opposed the concept of a flat earth.

10 *Guardian,* June 1, 2015

11 Source: NASA.

12 G-77 actually consists of 134 countries. It may have been only 77 at one time, but some wags have said that the name was adopted to contrast with the G-7, which consists of the EU, and Canada, France, Germany, Italy, Japan, the United Kingdom, and the United States.

13 *Aljazeera,* November 28, 2014 Of course, the world energy market will be destabilized if renewable energies become more dominant. What Saudi Arabia and other oil producers are most concerned about is loss of revenue, not just destabilization of the market.

14 Heck and Rogers, 2014.

15 *climatedev.com,* November 18, 2014.

16 *whitehouse.gov,* November 12, 2014.

17 ABC News, November 14, 2014.

18 *climatedev.com,* November 18, 2014.

19 NPR, March 22, 2015

20 Associated Press, November 27, 2014.

21 *Climateprogress.org,* May 18, 2015

22 Sources: Energy Information Administration (historical
emissions); World Bank (population); BP Statistical Review of World Energy, June 2014 (energy sources).

23 "China is investing US$294 billion in renewables over the five years to 2015 (that's not a typo; it's 3% of China's GDP)." *Guardian,* February 5, 2015.

24 Pri.org, September 21, 2015.

25 *Business Insider,* September 25, 2015.

26 business-standard.com, November 24, 2014.

27 Ibid.

28 *New York Times,* June 30, 2015.

29 *Science,* September 27, 2015.

30 Ibid.

31 Chasek et.al, 2013.

32 *Guardian,* December 28, 2014.

33 *Times of India,* January 22, 2015.

34 *New York Times,* January 27, 2015.

35 *New York Times,* November 17, 2014.

36 *New York Times,* December 3, 2015.

37 *Financial Times,* November 16, 2015. The G20 is a group of 20 large economies whose leaders meet periodically to discuss major global issues.

38 *climatedev.com,* November 18, 2014.

39 Ibid.

40 Stern, 2015

41 *Washington Post,* April 15, 2015

42 Ibid.

43 *New York Times,* November 10, 2015.

44 *Washington Post,* January 24, 2015.

45 rtcc.org, May 19, 2014.

46 *Forbes,* March 3, 2015.

47 *The Hindu,* January 23, 2015.

48 *Financial Times,* November 19, 2014.

49 Reuters, February 5, 2015.

50 Russian President Vladimir Putin reportedly believes that "there is no global warming, that this is a fraud to restrain the industrial development of several countries including Russia," according to Stanislav Belkovsky, a political analyst and critic of Putin. *Washington Post,* November 9, 2015.

51 *Sydney Morning Herald,* November 16, 2014.

52 Ibid.

53 *Guardian,* November 16, 2014.

54 Radio Canada International, November 15, 2014.

55 CBC, June 9, 2014. Harper's view on climate change has been characterized as follows: "his approach to climate issues mirrored the Bush-Cheney agenda: undermine the science, defer meaningful actions to rein in carbon dioxide emissions, and accelerate oil-and-gas development as quickly as possible." Cushman, 2014. Harper lost the 2015 parliamentary election and his successor, Justin Trudeau, seems more likely to support the Paris agreement.

56 McPherson, 2015.

57 *Guardian,* November 21, 2014.

58 Ibid.

59 *Washington Post,* November 12, 2014.

60 Agence France Press, November 12, 2014.

61 CNN November 12, 2014. Despite McConnell's opposition, some politicians applauded the action. "Now there is no longer an excuse for Congress to block action on climate change," said former Senate Environment and Public Works Chair Barbara Boxer (D-CA). "The biggest carbon polluter on our planet, China, has agreed to cut back on dangerous emissions, and now we should make sure all countries do their part because this is a threat to the people that we all represent." House Minority Leader Nancy Pelosi (D-CA) said, the agreement is "a commitment to confronting climate change with the seriousness it requires." She continued, "There is no excuse left for inaction…We must come together and take bold and ambitious steps to avert the climate crisis before us."

62 Brookings.com, November 25, 2014.

63 The Republican reaction to the U.S.-China agreement evoked some humor: Jonathan Chait's New York Magazine headline was, "China Tries to Save Earth; Republicans Furious." Andy Borowitz did a satirical piece for the New Yorker, headed "Republicans Demand Return of Passive Obama." It mocked House Speaker John Boehner and Senate Majority Leader Mitch

McConnell by pretending that they accused Obama of "engaging in a flagrant display of leadership that we find deeply offensive." Griffin, 2015.

64 Press release, March 31, 2015, mcconnell.senate.gov/public/.

65 *Atlantic,* December 1, 2015.

66 McConnell does not represent all Republicans. Senator Lindsey Graham (R-SC) has countered: "You know, when it comes to climate change being real, people of my party are all over the board. I said that it's real, that man has contributed to it in a substantial way. I think the Republican Party has to do some soul searching." *Bloomberg News,* March 24, 2015

67 *The Hill,* June 16, 2015

68 McConnell Press release, March 31, 2015, mcconnell.senate.gov/public/. On another occasion, McConnell said "The President's international negotiating partners at that conference should proceed with caution before entering into an unattainable deal with this administration, because commitments the president makes there would rest on a house of cards of his own making." *New York Times,* December 2, 2015.

69 *Huffington Post,* November 12, 2014.

70 *Wall Street Journal,* November 27, 2015.

71 *Los Angeles Times,* November 14, 2014.

72 *Wall Street Journal,* November 27, 2015.

73 Canada.com, November 20, 2014.

74 Instead, he continued to maintain, "climate change has been occurring since the beginning of time," and punctuated his claim by throwing a snowball on the Senate floor during the snowy February of 2015. With these antics, Inhofe used his role as a buffoon to caricature science. *Politico,* February 26, 2015. One commentator detected irony in his antics: "Now, global warming skepticism skeptics might argue that Inhofe, the author of a book about global warming called *The Greatest Hoax*, is using one bit of weather-related data to try to disprove a well-established, very long-term trend. They might note that temperatures in February are

supposed to be cold in the Northern Hemisphere since it is a season called 'winter.' They might point out that at the same time D.C. was very cold, the West Coast was very warm, which is less expected during 'winter.' And they might note that the government did indeed declare 2014 to be the warmest year on record, a detail that is not disproven by a snowball in the year 2015. (The sad irony of that, though: Much of the eastern U.S. recorded colder than normal temperatures -- and that is where Inhofe goes to work.) But those skepticism skeptics are wrong. Why? Look at that snowball." *Washington Post,* February 26, 2015.

75 *The Hill,* November 16, 2014.

76 ABC News, July 23, 2010. Inhofe does have a small kernel of truth for his misstatement: over a very long time scale, the globe will cool and enter a new ice age only if natural factors are considered. But with human influences, the globe is warming. "We do expect the natural trend to be a slow, 90,000-year cooling into the depths of a new ice age, but the globally averaged rate of cooling over that time would be something around 0.01 degree per century, and maybe three to four times bigger in the polar regions, where changes are largest. Human-induced changes are likely to be one hundred or more times faster, so the next natural ice age won't save us from ourselves." Alley, 2014.

77 Source: www.ncdc.noaa.gov/sotc/global/2014/13. While this data is acknowledged by "lukewarmers," it is downplayed: "The atmosphere isn't warming nearly as fast as is predicted in the forecasts that serve as the basis for some of the most onerous environmental regulations ever proposed (and adopted). In fact, you might say, instead of dramatic warming, lower atmospheric temperatures are lukewarming." Michaels and Knappenberger, 2015.

78 *New York Times,* October 21, 2015.

79 One can get a flavor of Inhofe's ideology from this tongue-in-cheek quote: "Oklahoma senator James Inhofe … insisted that the whole idea of human-driven climate

change was a hoax perpetrated on a gullible populace as a kind of stalking horse for a left-wing plot to turn the whole country into a dystopian, socialistic hellscape like Cuba or, worse, like Ithaca, New York." McGraw, 2015

80 Romm, 2015.

81 U.S. politicians at all levels have had problems recognizing climate science. In Florida, Governor Rick Scott's administration has apparently ruled out climate science: "Kristina Trotta, a former employee of the DEP [Department of Environmental Protection], told the Florida Center for Investigative Reporting that she and her colleagues were told not to use the terms "climate change" or "global warming," or, more broadly, "we were told that we were not allowed to discuss anything that was not a true fact."" CNN, March 9, 2015. If honestly applied, this policy would rule out such non-facts as "the globe is cooling" or "humans do not cause climate change." Local officials do not follow the state's lead because they have to deal with the consequences of climate change. Courtney Barker, city manager of Satellite Beach, said "For us, it's a reality, it's not a political issue. When you have to listen to that mantra, 'climate change, is it real or not?' you kind of chuckle because you see it." AP, May 11, 2015

Wisconsin, however, did followed Florida's lead: Wisconsin's Board of Commissioners of Public Lands voted 2-to-1 to prohibit staff "from engaging in global warming or climate change work," according to Huffingtonpost.com, April 9, 2015. One of the commissioners, Doug LaFollette (great-grandson of Robert LaFollette), voted against the ban and responded "The big important thing here is the attitude and the trend of public officials who, either out of ignorance or out of political expediency, deny the climate issue." *New York Times,* April 10, 2015

82 MSNBC, November 12, 2014.

83 Ibid.

84 *New York Times,* November 12, 2014.

85 Heartland Institute does more than fund denial conferences. Just before the Paris conference, Heartland launched a money-raising effort to fund "Pandemonium in Paris." In its statement on Indiegogo.com, a crowdfunding site, Heartland stated: "One of the most important battles in the history of the global warming debate will be fought this December at a United Nations climate conference in Paris. The UN is attempting to impose binding carbon dioxide restrictions on the United States and transfer billions of dollars of climate "reparations" from the United States to nations like Iran, North Korea, and Venezuela. It's called COP-21 – the twenty-first meeting of the Conference of the Parties to the UN Framework Convention on Climate Change. The Heartland Institute is working with other leading think tanks and advocacy groups to make sure our voice – the voice of sound science and economics, of energy consumers and taxpayers in America – is heard. We need your help us stop the UN and the Obama administration from raising your taxes, increasing your energy costs, and destroying jobs – perhaps your job or those of your children… We plan to send a delegation of scientists and policy experts to Paris to hold a 'counter-conference' during COP-21 to demonstrate there is strong and informed opposition to Obama's plans and to expose the agendas and true costs of the agreement being negotiated there." Indiegogo.com, November 13, 2015.

86 *Washington Post*, November 12, 2014.

87 *Dallas Morning News*, November 12, 2014.

88 *Washington Post*, November 12, 2014.

89 http://thinkprogress.org/climate/
2015/07/26/3683808/gop-field-climate-energy-ranked/

90 While denial ideologues emphasize economic damage from instituting climate policies, they ignore the damage caused by inaction. In one model, the damage caused by an increase of 75% in CO2 emissions during the next 85 years would amount to about $370 trillion. "The model assumed that human activities by themselves would boost carbon dioxide levels 75% from today to 2100. Total

damages without the permafrost emissions would be $326 trillion globally, the researchers found. With permafrost-related emissions included, however, additional damages ranged from $3 trillion to $166 trillion, depending on how much human emissions warmed the Arctic, the team reports online today in Nature Climate Change; the average value was $43 trillion." *Science,* September 21, 2015.

91 McPherson, 2014.

92 *Guardian,* December 28, 2014.

93 Chasek, et.al, 2013.

94 *New York Times,* November 12, 2015.

95 One prominent climate science denier, Marc Morano, suggested that a Republican president would retract support for a Paris agreement and EPA regulations: "Climate activists also know that if a Republican wins the presidency in 2016, any potential U.N. Climate Treaty and the EPA climate regulations may face dismantling." Wnd.com, March 22, 2015.

96 *New York Times,* November 12, 2014.

97 *Guardian,* January 15, 2015.

98 Thinkprogress.org, July 8, 2015. Emphasis in original.

99 Thinkprogress.org, October 21, 2015.

100 Ibid.

101 thinkprogress.org, November 19, 2015.

102 *New York Times,* December 2, 2015.

103 *New York Times,* December 4, 2015.

104 McPherson, 2015.

105 Unfortunately, when politicians do speak about extreme weather, it sometimes means that they deny any role of climate change. When the Federal Emergency Management Agency (FEMA) asked states to plan for climate change induced weather disasters, two senators from one of the most vulnerable states, Louisiana, wrote a letter to FEMA with the following statement: "We are concerned FEMA's recent decision to require States to address climate change in their mitigation strategies injects unnecessary, ideological-based red tape into the disaster preparedness process. Planning and preparing for

disasters should be focused on strengthening and protecting local communities from inevitable weather events and not about falling in line with the President's political agenda." Nola.com, May 5, 2015.

106 *Carbon Pollution Emission Guidelines for Existing Stationary Sources: Electric Utility Generating Units; 40 CFR Part 60. Carbon Pollution* is an interesting term that is used legally to refer to carbon dioxide emissions. Some denial ideologues regard it as a misnomer: "There is no such thing as carbon pollution and the carbon gas emitted from industry is CO2 – a colourless, odourless, non-toxic gas. CO2 is plant food. It is good for life on Earth, and human emissions are directly proportional to employment. There is a very low level of the community scientific knowledge displayed when CO2 is regarded as a pollutant rather than the key to photosynthesis." Plimer in Abbott et.al, 2015. This statement, and many others like it made by denial ideologues, implies that increases in CO2 are not of concern for climate change, a canard refuted by 97% of climate scientists. Some denial ideologues will claim that temperature increases related to CO2 emissions increases are minor and decrease with each doubling of CO2 concentrations, another canard. See McPherson, 2015, for a full discussion of this topic.
107 Denial ideology converts EPA rules into buzzwords such as *war on coal:* "a central target in the Obama administration's all-out war on fossil fuels is the coal industry. The real casualties of that war will be businesses, jobs and household energy budgets, with few if any public health benefits." Bell, 2015.
108 *The Hill,* March 5, 2015.
109 Ibid.
110 "Section 111 of the Clean Air Act provides for the establishment of nationwide emission standards for major stationary sources of dangerous air pollution including, since 1971, power plants. In response to the Supreme Court's decision in Massachusetts v. EPA that the Clean Air Act's protections encompass greenhouse gas

emissions and to EPA's science based determination that these climate-destabilizing emissions endanger public health and welfare,…EPA is developing separate carbon pollution-reduction frameworks for new and existing power plants under Clean Air Act § 111(b) and (d) respectively." Megan Ceronsky & Tomás Carbonell *Section 111(d) of the Clean Air Act: The Legal Foundation for Strong, Flexible & Cost-Effective Carbon Pollution Standards for Existing Power Plants,* Environmental Defense Fund, October 2013 (revised February 2014).

111 *New York Times,* June 2, 2015.

112 Ibid.

113 Ibid.

114 Ibid.

115 David Doniger, air and climate director at the Natural Resources Defense Council, quoted in *The Hill,* July 12, 2015

116 *New York Times,* November 29, 2015.

117 *Guardian,* September 14, 2015.

118 *Washington Times,* April 18, 2015.

119 CBS, April 18, 2015.

120 *New York Times,* June 22, 2015. Health costs of climate change are contentious; some denial ideologues will argue that fossil fuel use promotes health because it alleviates poverty and other problems that lead to ill health. They do not accept findings that climate change increases death from heat waves, droughts, floods or other consequences. They defend the use of coal as a means of alleviating poverty. Coal executives even argue that coal can be "healthy": National Mining Association spokesman Luke Popovich said, "it makes far more sense to support the technologies that make coal cleaner to use than to support policies that would deny its use to those who rightfully want the comforts of civilization." *New York Times,* June 22, 2015. "Comforts of civilization" is a euphemism for wealth, which is presumably healthier than poverty. Political leaders have echoed this view. Senator Marco Rubio (R-FL) said "But I also believe it's

in the common good to protect our economy. There are people all over this planet and in this country who have emerged from poverty in large respect because of the availability of affordable energy. It creates industries. It makes the cost of living lower. And we have to take that into account as well." *Huffington Post,* June 22, 2015.

121 *Washington Post,* November 15, 2014.

122 At times, denial ideologues' rejection of EPA authority goes beyond the actual legislative history to invent a rationale for denying EPA authority on climate change: "Over the past three decades the Congress not only has never passed any legislation to regulate climate change, but has specifically rejected legislation to give EPA the authority which it now claims." Bell, 2015. This flies in the face of the fact that Congress did include climate in the Clean Air Act, which explicitly contains the word "climate" in its definition of pollutant. McPherson, 2014.

123 *Washington Times,* November 17, 2014.

124 http://www.theage.com.au/comment. Hollande is clearly concerned about the success of the Paris COP, as he later indicated in a statement about Syrian refugees: "There is a risk of failure. If we don't conclude [with a successful agreement], and there are no substantial measures to ensure the transition [to a climate-affected world], it won't be hundreds of thousands of refugees in the next 20 years, it will be millions." *Guardian,* September 7, 2015. A number of European leaders have expressed concern about success of the Paris COP because they consider the refugee crisis a part of climate change. The Syrian drought contributed to the conflict there as many rural residents were forced into cities when crops failed, and the cities became hotbeds of rebellion.

125 http://www4.unfccc.int/submissions/INDC/ Published%20Documents/United%20States%20of%20A merica/1/U.S.%20Cover%20Note%20INDC%20and%20 Accompanying%20Information.pdf

126 ENB Vol.12, Lima Climate Change Conference, Dec. 2014.

(NOTE: ENB refers to Earth Negotiations Bulletin)

127 NPR, December 4, 2014.

128 UNFCCC.int, "COP-20 Climate Change, the New Economy".

129 Ibid.

130 Ibid.

131 "The country has 43 coal-fired power plants either planned or under construction, according to Bloomberg. If built, those plants would have a combined carbon footprint equal to 10 percent of Japan's current total emissions, and equal to 50 percent of the total emissions it aims to have in 2050. Even now, the country's coal consumption is on the rise, and its emissions in 2013, the year for which the most recent data is available, were the second-highest on record." *Mother Jones,* April 28, 2015

132 Ibid.

133 *Guardian,* October 17, 2014.

134 *Guardian,* December 2, 2014.

135 *New York Times,* November 13, 2015.

136 *Guardian,* July 15, 2015

137 Climate Action Tracker analyzed the commitments by UNFCCC member parties and concluded: "Current policies place the world on a path towards 3.6 to 4.2°C warming above pre-industrial levels, whereas the unconditional pledges or promises that governments have made, as of early 2015, would limit warming to 2.9 to 3.1°C above pre-industrial levels. In other words, there is still a substantial gap between what governments have promised to do and the total level of actions they have undertaken to date. Both the current policy and pledge trajectories lie well above emissions pathways consistent with a 1.5°C or 2°C world."

http://climateactiontracker.org/global.html

It remains to be seen if the pledges made during 2015 can "bend the curve" enough to reach the 2C goal.

138 *Wall Street Journal,* December 2, 2014.

139 Ibid.

140 AP, December 15, 2014.

141 In the months before negotiation of the Kyoto Protocol in December 1997, the Clinton administration miscalculated that the U.S. delegates could overcome CBDR problems with a provision called the "Clean Development Mechanism (CDM). CDM permits developed countries to invest in emissions reduction projects in developing countries and receive credit for their own emissions targets. But the adoption of CDM did not lead to the desired goal: "In an effort to break the impasse over differentiation, the United States was willing to establish a new system that would foster investments in clean energy projects and the protection of forests in developing countries. The Clinton administration calculated that perhaps, in return, key developing countries would agree to set goals of their own. That hope was promptly dashed. The developing countries were glad to accept the help but not the condition. National targets, they feared, would limit their growth and infringe on their sovereignty." (Talbott and Antholis, 2011)

142 Chasek et.al, 2013.

143 Ibid.

144 BBC, December 12, 2014.

145 EDF.org, January 5, 2014. Emphasis in original.

146 McPherson, 2015.

147 *The Diplomat,* December 17, 2014.

148 ENB Vol.12, Lima Climate Change Conference, Dec. 2014.

149 Ibid.

150 AP, December 15, 2014.

151 Bell, 2015.

152 McPherson, 2015.

153 *New York Times,* November 10, 2015.

154 Welzer, 2015

155 *Guardian,* February 4, 2014.

156 *The Hill,* November 2, 2015.

157 ENB Vol.12, Lima Climate Change Conference, Dec. 2014.

158 Submission to UNFCCC, October 2014.

159 ENB Vol.12, Lima Climate Change Conference, Dec. 2014.

160 BBC, December 12, 2014.

161 ENB Vol.12, Lima Climate Change Conference, Dec. 2014.

162 *Guardian*, December 11, 2014.

163 *Guardian*, December 12, 2014.

164 http://unfccc.int/files/essential_background/background_ publications_htmlpdf/application/pdf/conveng.pdf

165 Simeon Tegel, *Globalpost*, December 10, 2014.

166 McPherson, 2015.

167 ENB Vol.12, Lima Climate Change Conference, Dec. 2014.

168 Ibid.

169 *Guardian*, October 30, 2015.

170 c2es.org, December 18, 2014.

171 Reuters, December 15, 2014.

172 The Green Climate Fund came out of the 2009 Copenhagen COP-15, where parties pledged $100 billion.

173 ENB Vol.12, Lima Climate Change Conference, Dec. 2014.

174 Ibid.

175 Ibid.

176 ENB Vol.12, Lima Climate Change Conference, Dec. 2014.

177 *Guardian*, December 12, 2014.

178 *Guardian*, December 11, 2014.

179 Carlin goes further and says that developing countries are unconvinced of the threats of climate change, particularly extreme weather, and that causes an impasse over financing. "The failure of the developed world to argue against the views of many less developed countries concerning the alleged effects of CO2 emissions on extreme and unusual weather has resulted in an unnecessary additional impasse between the developed and less developed worlds over 'compensation' for the damages of such weather events allegedly caused by developed world CO2 emissions. Obama's decision to

very publicly endorse EWD, despite the absence of any scientific basis for it, appears to have contributed to this push by less developed countries." Carlin, 2015. In Carlin's jargon, EWD refers to Extreme Weather Doctrine. This conflates the issue of financing with the issue of causation of extreme weather. Regardless, Carlin goes on to repeat the old saw that climate agreements are part of a scheme to redistribute world income: "Could it be that the less developed countries are trying to use CAGW and EWD science as the basis for world income redistribution at the expense of the developed countries?" Ibid. He concludes that developing countries, who do not believe climate science, are not likely to comply with any commitments under the Paris agreement: "The idea that these countries will agree to actually reduce energy use because the US may reduce its CO2 emissions through EPA regulations because of UN reports they have never heard of is ridiculous." Ibid. I am not sure how he knows that developing countries have "never heard of" IPCC reports, which are featured at every meeting of the UNFCCC that they attend.

180 *The Diplomat,* December 17, 2014.
181 Ibid.
182 Carlin, 2015.
183 *New York Times,* November 23, 2015.
184 Dailysignal.com, November 18, 2015.
185 *Guardian,* December 12, 2014.
186 *New York Times,* December 14, 2014.
187 Ibid.
188 *The Globe and Mail,* December 28, 2014.
189 Member parties who have not submitted ambitious INDCs are not encouraged to do so by the statements of U.S. politicians. "Other countries are catching on, which is reflected by the fact that such a small amount of countries have submitted intended nationally determined contributions with only a few months to go," said Senator James Inhofe (R-OK). *Wall Street Journal,* August 23, 2015. Inhofe is referring to the possibility that Congress and future U.S. presidents might not support a Paris

agreement or continue to carry out the pledges made by the Obama administration.

190 *Guardian,* January 15, 2015.

191 Thinkprogress.org, September 25, 2015.

192 *Cornwall Alliance Newsletter, April 25, 2015.* Emphasis in original. In addition to Cornwall Alliance, another denial organization, Heartland Institute, weighed in on the pope's climate stance: "Though Pope Francis's heart is surely in the right place, he would do his flock and the world a disservice by putting his moral authority behind the United Nations' unscientific agenda on the climate." Joseph Bast, Heartland's president, quoted in *New York Times,* April 27, 2015.

193 McPherson, 2014, 2015. In a newsletter, Cornwall Alliance has tried to equate economic development, alleviation of poverty and CO2 emissions as though all would proceed in lock-step: "Economic theory and economic history, coupled with the physics and engineering of energy production and distribution, strongly suggest that decoupling economic development from CO2 emissions is, now and for the foreseeable future, not possible… Make energy more expensive, and its consumption will decline, and therefore so also will the production of everything else we produce, i.e., people will either not rise out of poverty or will fall back toward or into it." Cornwallalliance.org, August 21, 2015, emphasis in original.

194 Oil companies have recognized that climate change threatens their business. While some have acknowledged climate science in public, they continue to fund denial ideologues in secret. This has led the Union of Concerned Scientists to issue a report in July 2015 on "Climate Deception Dossiers" with these two recommendations (among others): "In addition to ceasing the spread of misinformation, fossil fuel companies should also:

    • Support fair and cost-effective policies to reduce global-warming emissions. The fossil fuel industry has generally opposed a wide array of policies, including carbon pricing, cap-and-trade, renewable energy standards, renewable fuel standards, direct emission regulation, and others. It is time for the industry to identify and publicly support policies that will lead to the reduction of emissions at a scale needed to lessen the worst effects of global warming...

• Pay for their share of the costs of climate damages and preparedness. Communities around the world are already facing and paying for damages from rising seas, extreme heat, more frequent droughts, and other climate-related impacts. Additional investments must be made to protect and prepare communities for these risks today and in the future, and fossil fuel companies should pay a fair share of the costs." If the fossil fuel companies did indeed pay for costs of climate damages, it would go a long way toward fulfilling the "loss and damage" provisions of the COP21 decision. However, they are reluctant to open themselves to massive lawsuits that might come from following this recommendation. See Chapter 5 for details on the "loss and damage" decision.

195 *Cornwall Alliance Newsletter,* September 21, 2015.
196 MSNBC, September 18, 2015. The pope was not very emphatic in his address to Congress. He repeated a phrase from *Laudato Si* which made reference to human impact on the environment: "In *Laudato Si'*, I call for a courageous and responsible effort to 'redirect our steps' and to avert the most serious effects of the environmental deterioration caused by human activity. I am convinced that we can make a difference and I have no doubt that the United States – and this Congress – have an important role to play." *New York Times,* September 24, 2015. He did not emphasize the Paris agreement, however.
Not all Republicans have problems with addressing climate change. Some get "religion" when their districts are affected. Congressman Carlos Curbelo (R-FL) said, "South Florida is the frontline of climate change, where we have seen its negative impact in the form of rising sea-levels and the erosion of our coastal communities. In Miami-Dade County alone, more people live less than a

mere four feet above sea level than any state in the union with the exception of Florida and Louisiana. In fact, 40% of Florida's population is at risk of rising sea levels, posing a clear and present danger. Our goal with this resolution is to shift the debate from whether climate change is real to what we can do to mitigate its effects." Curbelo was speaking about a House resolution sponsored by 11 House Republicans to "study and address the causes and effects of measured changes to our global and regional climates."
http://gibson.house.gov/news/
197 Carlin, 2015.
198 McPherson, 2015.
199 *Financial Times,* December 7, 2014.
200 Some world leaders have argued that fossil-fuel subsidies increase global warming by raising the rate of fossil fuel use. Prince Charles spoke about this at a meeting of the Cambridge Institute for Sustainability Leadership: "In his speech the prince also noted that abolishing fossil fuel subsidies, estimated at $500bn (£320bn) a year by the International Energy Agency (IEA), would cut global carbon emissions by 13%."
Guardian, July 2, 2015
201 Sir Nicholas Stern has identified the problem: "The IEA's World Energy Outlook 2012 estimated that only around 30% of global proved fossil fuel reserves can be burned uncaptured between 2012 and 2050 if the world is to maintain a 2 ° C path…. The world is not facing up to this basic logic. It is not consistent to believe that the 2 ° C target can be achieved if fossil fuel reserves have their current value attributed to them." Stern, 2015.
202 *Guardian,* March 10, 2015.
203 *Guardian,* December 23, 2014.
204 Stern, 2015.
205 BBC, March 6, 2014.
206 McPherson, 2014.
207 *The Hill,* December 8, 2014. Emphasis added.
208 *Rolling Stone,* December 29, 2014.
209 *Cornwall Alliance Newsletter,* December 19, 2014.

210 For a full discussion of this issue see Stern, 2015.

211 More details are available in McPherson, 2014.

212 AP, December 14, 2014.

213 Ibid.

214 *New York Times,* December 14, 2014.

215 *Bloomberg View,* December 22, 2014.

216 McPherson, 2015.

217 ENB Vol.12, Lima Climate Change Conference, Dec. 2014.

218 Ibid.

219 Chasek et.al, 2013.

220 McPherson, 2014.

221 Chasek, et.al, 2013 .

222 The IPCC has been a steady source of science in the international monitoring of climate change, but it has also been subject to political pressures. When the scandal over Exxon's suppression of climate science erupted in the U.S. in November 2015, it was revealed that Exxon had used its connections in the Bush administration to get the then-chairman, Bob Watson, removed from the IPCC bureau. "Exxon's senior environmental adviser in Washington sent a memo to Bush's Council on Environmental Quality demanding the removal of both Mike MacCracken, who coordinated the first National Climate Assessment, and Bob Watson, the chairman of the IPCC. Both scientists were gone from their positions within a year." *The Hill,* November 10, 2015.

223 https://www.wmo.int/pages/mediacentre/

224 I had the opportunity to report on side events for ENB during the Barcelona intersessional meeting in 2009.

225 ENB Volume 12, Number 620.

226 ENB Vol. 12 February 16, 2015.

227 *Guardian,* January 7, 2015.

228 Ibid.

229 *Guardian,* February 21, 2015.

230 ENB Vol. 12 February 11, 2015.

231 ENB Vol. 12 February 16, 2015.

232 climatecentral.org, February 10, 2015.

233 *New York Times,* February 13, 2015.

234 "We have come to Geneva with a clear objective of working towards adopting a legally binding agreement at COP 21 that is capable of keeping us collectively on track to achieve the below 2°C objective." adp2-8_opening_statement_eu_8feb2015.pdf, available at http://unfccc.int/bodies/awg/items/7544.php Some observers who deny the need for a climate agreement have characterized the EU position as follows: "The EU on the other hand wanted to use the arena of the UN climate conferences to ratchet forward progress toward its goal of having a legally binding treaty ready for the Paris COP at the end of 2015. This involved cajoling, bribing—with promises of climate funding—and pressuring developing countries toward a destination they didn't want to reach." Darwall in Abbott et.al, 2015.

235 *Guardian,* February 23, 2015.

236 Source: http://data.worldbank.org/indicator/EN.ATM.CO2E.PC

237 Griffin, 2015. China and India will become much more significant in calculations about emissions reductions. Depending on how fast their economies, populations, and energy usage increase, China and India could, by themselves, put as many gigatons of CO2 and other greenhouse gases into the atmosphere as the developed countries are now pledging to cut. China and India could even exceed the 15-gigaton goal for the whole world in 2050. In fact, even if one of the two giants participated fully and the other stayed out, the very difficult task of bringing global annual CO2 emissions down to 15 gigatons by 2050 would be unattainable." Talbott and Antholis, 2011.

238 McPherson, 2015.

239 Heinberg, 2015. Living standards in developed countries such as the U.S. are sometimes profligate in ways that make adjusting to climate change difficult, even if there are viable alternatives that would keep prosperity at current levels while reducing emissions. An example is sprawl, which affects not only emissions from

transportation but also resources that are used to support large households. In California, the severe drought (McPherson, 2015) required the state government to impose restrictions on water use. One city official, Tom Gray, the general manager of the Fair Oaks Water District, complained that "it did not seem fair to determine [limits] based on per capita use when his district is in a suburban area where people have larger lots than in urban areas, and thus residents naturally use more water." *New York Times,* April 10, 2015. Of course, those residents could find housing with smaller lots or no lots at all if cities discouraged sprawl and developers used land more efficiently.

240 ENB Vol. 12 February 8, 2015.

241 Brazil is suffering one of the consequences of development, exacerbated by worldwide climate change: severe drought. As the Amazon rain forest is denuded for agricultural development, rains have become less frequent and reservoirs have dried up. Sao Paolo has suffered an extreme drought in 2015, the worst in nearly a century. *New York Times,* February 16, 2015.

242 ENB, Vol. 12, February 16, 2015.

243 Reuters, May 31, 2015.

244 Ibid.

245 *Guardian*, June 1, 2015.

246 ENB Vol. 12 No. 635.

247 ENB Vol. 12 No. 629.

248 *Guardian,* June 3, 2015.

249 *New York Times,* September 28, 2015.

250 Ibid.

251 Reuters, June 1, 2015.

252 *New York Times,* June 11, 2015

253 *Green Business*, June 8, 2015.

254 ENB Vol. 12 No. 632.

255 *Toronto Star,* June 8, 2015.

256 Pope Francis, encyclical letter *Laudato Si*. People sometimes misunderstand the science and confuse annual emissions with concentrations, which build up over time. We know from Keeling's research that concentrations

have increased since 1958 from about 320 ppm to 400 ppm, albeit varying in how much is added each year. An example of misunderstanding CO2 concentrations: "In the last 3 decades carbon in US air has reduced by nearly 50%," according to Rupert Murdoch (CNN, August 27, 2015). Murdoch is incorrect on two facts: US carbon dioxide emissions have grown, not "reduced;" and "carbon in US air" is increasing along with worldwide emissions. Even if the U.S. did reduce its rate of emissions (which it has done recently, but not for 30 years), carbon would still increase from overseas emissions. CO2 knows no boundaries.

257 Ibid.

258 AP, June 19, 2015.

259 *Huffington Post,* June 12, 2015.

260 *New York Times,* June 16, 2015.

261 Ibid.

262 Some have gone further and have accused the pope of paganism: "The Heartland Institute's marketing director, Gene Koprowski, actually said that he and his colleagues believe the Pope is motivated by 'pagan remnants' of 'nature worship' reasserting themselves in the Catholic Church." Thinkprogress.org, September 21, 2015. This accusation fits a pattern of denial ideologues' denigration of climate science as a nature religion. McPherson, 2015.

263 time.com, June 17, 2015.

264 *New York Times,* September 25, 2015.

265 An interesting historical analysis has documented disproportional effects of economic growth and prosperity in the "First World" on poverty and mortality in "Third World" nations. When European and the U.S. growth surged in the 19th century, many parts of Asia, Africa and Latin America suffered from droughts and other climate effects caused by industrialization and land use changes. Brooke, 2014.

266 http://unfccc.int/resource/docs/2015/ adp2/eng/4infnot.pdf

267 ENB Vol. 12 No. 640 - Bonn Climate Change Conference

268 ENB Vol. 12 No. 641 - Bonn Climate Change Conference.

269 *Guardian,* September 7, 2015.

270 *Guardian,* September 3, 2015.

271 Climatecentral.org, November 11, 2015.

272 ENB Vol. 12 No. 642 - Bonn Climate Change Conference

273 *Time,* September 3, 2015.

274 Ibid.

275 *Washington Examiner,* September 6, 2015.

276 ENB Vol. 12 No. 644 - Bonn Climate Change Conference

277 ADP.2015.8.InformalNote on the UNFCCC.int web site

278 ENB Vol. 12 No. 647 - Bonn Climate Change Conference - October 2015 - Issue #2.

279 ENB Vol. 12 No. 647 - Bonn Climate Change Conference - October 2015- Summary.

280 Ibid.

281 ENB Vol. 12 No. 647 - Bonn Climate Change Conference - October 2015 - Issue #2.

282 The difference between 1.5 and 2 degrees is not insignificant. "At 1.5 degrees of warming, global GDP is expected to fall by $20 trillion. At 2.5 degrees, the economic damage is estimated at $44 trillion. And if the world reaches 4.5 degrees of warming – a level some scientists say we're on pace to reach – the economic carnage would top out at $72 trillion." MSNBC, October 29, 2015.

283 Ibid.

284 BBC News, October 23, 2015.

285 *New York Times,* October 25, 2015.

286 ENB Vol. 12 No. 647 - Bonn Climate Change Conference - October 2015 - Issue #2.

287 An interesting sideline issue is the use of domestic law to pursue fossil fuel companies. A group of Native Americans in Alaska has sued energy companies, and there is discussion of bringing a lawsuit against Exxon-Mobil for its deceptive use of denial after its scientists

showed that its carbon emissions would cause climate change. See thinkprogress.org, October 20, 2015.

288 BBC News, October 23, 2015.

289 ENB Vol. 12 No. 647 - Bonn Climate Change Conference - October 2015 - Issue #4.

290 CFACT is the Committee for a Constructive Tomorrow, a conservative Washington, D.C.-based non-profit organization. It is a member organization of the Cooler Heads Coalition, which aims at "dispelling the myths of global warming through science and analysis." Sources: wnd.com, November 1, 2015, Wikipedia.com.

291 Romm, 2015,

292 *Washington Times,* November 19, 2015.

293 *Cornwall Alliance Newsletter,* November 16, 2015.

294 Ibid.

295 Ibid.

296 politico.com, January 7, 2015.

297 *USA Today,* April 21, 2015. *Time,* October 19, 2015.

298 *Guardian,* July 6, 2015

299 ENB Vol. 12 No. 652 - Paris Climate Change Conference - November 2015 - Issue #1.

300 Ibid.

301 *New York Times,* November 30, 2015.

302 Ibid.

303 ENB Vol. 12 No. 653 - Paris Climate Change Conference - November 2015 - Issue #2.

304 Ibid.

305 ENB Vol. 12 No. 654 - Paris Climate Change Conference - November 2015 - Issue #3.

306 Ibid.

307 ENB Vol. 12 No. 655 - Paris Climate Change Conference - November 2015 - Issue #4.

308 ENB Vol. 12 No. 656 - Paris Climate Change Conference - November 2015 - Issue 5.

309 *New York Times,* November 29, 2015.

310 *New York Times,* November 30, 2015.

311 ENB Vol. 12 No. 656 - Paris Climate Change Conference - November 2015 - Issue 5.

312 Ibid.

313 *New York Times,* December 2, 2015.

314 democracynow.org, December 12, 2015.

315 *New York Times,* December 14, 2015.

316 *Wall Street Journal,* December 14, 2015.

317 Michaels and Knappenberger, 2015.

318 *Cornwall Alliance Newsletter,* December 14, 2015.

319 Foxnews.com, December 7, 2015.

320 Vox.com, December 2, 2015.

321 CBS News, December 3, 2015.

322 Michaels and Knappenberger, 2015.

323 *Wall Street Journal,* March 20, 2015.

324 *Guardian,* March 26, 2015.

325 http://ec.europa.eu/clima/policies/g-gas/index_en.htm

326 Stern notes that making an agreement legally binding may moderate ambition: "Focusing on making targets internationally legally binding, and subject to enforcement measures (however noncredible), can have the opposite effect of encouraging countries to moderate their ambition by making the lowest possible international commitment that they feel they can get away with, or that which they are very confident they can achieve." Stern, 2015.

327 IPCC 2013-14.

328 Sometimes these attacks are implicit in statements by politicians who suggest that climate scientists are not proving that climate change is dangerous. An example is Senator Marco Rubio (R-FL), a presidential candidate, who said "If we do the things they want us to do, cap-and-trade, you name it, how much will that change the pace of climate change versus how much will that cost to our economy? Scientists can't tell us what impact it would have on reversing these changes, but I can tell you with certainty, it would have a devastating impact on our economy." (*Washington Post,* April 19, 2015) While scientists may not "tell us what impact" a specific policy may have, they can certainly tell us the impact of no policy, and it is not good.

329 Lawson in Abbott et.al, 2015.

330 It is doubtful that the IPCC can have much effect on negotiations directly through its reports, but the scientific findings conveyed by these reports do influence governments to negotiate emissions limits. Nevertheless, denial ideology tends to blame IPCC for many presumed sins. Animus against the IPCC extends to so-called "agendas" that it purportedly foists upon governments: "IPCC Summary for Policymakers reports offer repeated prescriptions to carry out UN agendas aimed most particularly at redistributing American wealth in penance for our unfair capitalist free market prosperity." Bell, 2015.

331 *New York Times,* April 24, 2015.

332 *Vision for Paris: Building an Effective Climate Agreement*, July 2015, The Center for Climate and Energy Solutions.

333 *Guardian,* June 15, 2015.

334 *Wall Street Journal,* November 23, 2015.

335 Politico.com, November 23, 2015.

336 I was environment attaché at the U.S. Mission to UN agencies in Geneva from 1996 to 2000. I was a writer-editor for *Earth Negotiations Bulletin* from 2004 to 2010. I attended COP21 in Paris as a delegate with the Unitarian Universalist Association UN Office.

337 Cf. Biermann, 2014, Chasek et.al, 2013, Stevenson and Dryzek, 2014.

338 McPherson, 2015. Perhaps the metaphor of devil worship applies more appropriately to those who would put their faith in fossil fueled growth. Oil has been called "the devil's excrement" and images of hell include flames, perhaps from burning fossil fuels.

339 Ibid.

340 DiMento et.al, 2015

341 Irresponsibility on the part of multinational corporations is exacerbated by lack of international law governing their activities: "there is no international legal instrument regulating the environmental activities of transnational corporations; few agreements that prevent trade in products, semifinished products, and components

from unsustainable industries along transnational supply chains; no agreement that anticipates and seeks to manage the increasing physical volume of commodities produced and consumed; no agreement to assist the global movement of environmentally displaced persons; and no agreement to anticipate and regulate geoengineering." Christoff and Eckersley, 2013.

342 http://www.wri.org/ipcc-infographics

343 *New York Times,* November 28, 2015.

344 *New York Times,* November 10, 2015.

345 Ibid.

346 Ibid.

347 Christoff and Eckersley, 2013.

348 One would think that oil companies that realize that they cannot develop their reserves, or acknowledge the need for putting a price on carbon, would instead use their investment funds to develop renewable energies. "The Carbon Tracker Initiative, a financial thinktank, said oil companies were spending between 1%-2% of their research and development budget on renewable energies, a figure that had not changed in years." *Guardian,* October 16, 2015.

349 *Guardian,* June 1, 2015.

350 *New York Times,* December 4, 2015.

351 *New York Times,* October 16, 2015.

352 *Guardian,* October 16, 2015.

353 I use the term "dozen" to indicate that there were varying numbers, depending on the timeframe. For example, Australia did not ratify until 2007 and Canada dropped out in 2011. The EU was counted for MRV purposes as a single party.

354 Climatecentral.org, October 18, 2015.

355 Biermann, 2014.

356 Christoff and Eckersley, 2013.

357 Ibid.

358 McPherson, 2014.

359 McPherson, 2015.

360 Vince, 2014.

361 Chasek et.al, 2013.

362 Rick Santorum, Republican candidate for president in 2016, has challenged the scientific consensus: "The most recent survey of climate scientists said about 57 percent don't agree with the idea that 95 percent of the change in the climate is being caused by CO2." This figure was derived from a blog, *Fabius Maximus,* which misused survey results from a study by researchers in the Netherlands and Australia. The results of that survey were published in 2014 in the journal *Environmental Science & Technology.* The researchers said that Santorum did not accurately represent the study's findings, and reviewers found that *Fabius Maximus* had completely distorted the research by using faulty logic and inaccurate assumptions. See factcheck.org, September 2, 2015.

363 Howe, 2014.

364 McPherson, 2014, 2015.

365 Ibid.

366 Howe, 2014.

367 McPherson, 2015.

368 G20 includes Argentina, Australia, Brazil, Canada, China, France, Germany, India, Indonesia, Italy, Japan, Mexico, Russia, Saudi Arabia, South Africa, South Korea, Turkey, the United Kingdom and the United States, and the commission of the European Union (EU).

369 Biermann, 2014.

370 Compston and Bailey, 2013.

371 McPherson, 2015.

372 Talbott and Antholis, 2015.

373 Ibid.

374 *Guardian,* January 22, 2015.

375 *Rockford (IL) Register Star*, March 10, 2012. Perhaps Inhofe is unaware that the Bible does state that man can change the earth: "The time has come for judging the dead, and for rewarding your servants the prophets and your people who revere your name, both great and small – and for destroying those who destroy the earth." Revelations 11:18

376 The coal industry has been fighting back against climate science. "As the 'war on coal' continues, I trust

that the commitment we have made to support Chris Horner's work will eventually create great awareness of the illegal tactics being employed to pass laws that are intended to destroy our industry." Coal & Investment Leadership Forum, quoted in *The Intercept,* August 25, 2015. Chris Horner is a lawyer who has pushed for investigations of climate scientists affiliated with the Intergovernmental Panel on Climate Change and NASA.

377 *Rockford (IL) Register Star*, March 10, 2012.
378 Christoff and Eckersley, 2013.
379 Chasek et.al, 2013.
380 McPherson, 2015.
381 Chasek et.al, 2013.
382 Earth Negotiations Bulletin (ENB)
Volume 12 Number 649 | Thursday, 22 October 2015
383 *Wall Street Journal,* November 17, 2015.
384 Greer, 2011.
385 Brooke, 2015.
386 Pickett and Wilkinson, 2010.
387 Greer, 2011.
388 Pickett and Wilkinson, 2010.
389 Welzer, 2015.
390 *New York Times,* September 3, 2015.
391 Greer, 2011.
392 Carlin, 2015.
393 *New York Times,* June 18, 2015.
394 Ibid.
395 McPherson, 2014.
396 McPherson, 2015.
397 sindicatum.com, March 5, 2015.
398 Chasek, et.al, 2013.
399 Ibid.
400 Three useful sites are:
Household calculator:
http://www.nature.org/greenliving/carboncalculator/
Air travel calculator:
http://calculator.carbonfootprint.com/calculator.aspx?tab=3

Planet requirement calculator:
https://www.greencred.me/index.php
401 *Financial Times,* January 5, 2015.
402 *Guardian,* March 15, 2015.
403 Ibid.
404 The business press has been reporting on this topic:
"In February, Shell Chief Executive Ben van Beurden
told a group of executives decked out in tuxedos and
formal gowns at an oil and gas conference in London that
they could no longer keep a 'low profile on the issue' of
climate change ahead of United Nations-sponsored talks
in Paris this year that could result in new global carbon-
emissions limits. 'We have to make sure that our voice is
heard by members of government, by civil society and the
general public,' he said. The Vatican is another important
constituency. In an unusually explicit mix of the political
and pastoral, Pope Francis has said he wants his
encyclical about the environment to come out before the
Paris climate meeting, so that it can 'make a contribution'
to deliberations there. 'We have to stop being defensive,'
according to Total CEO Patrick Pouyanné." *Wall Street
Journal,* May 25, 2015
Another report came from Reuters: "Oil companies, while
acknowledging the need to address climate change risks,
have said it will take decades to develop technologies that
economically capture carbon emissions. In January,
Europe's Royal Dutch Shell Plc backed a measure from
activist investors asking it to be more proactive about
planning for climate change." *Reuters,* May 27, 2015
405 blogs.heartland.org, January 5, 2015.
406 Ibid.
407 McPherson, 2014.
408 Wood, 2013.
409 McPherson, 2015.
410 Wood, 2013.
411 Fensin, 2015.
412 Ibid.
413 e.g., Klein, 2014; Hansen, 2009; Hertsgaard, 2011;
Heck and Rogers, 2014.